Always Believe!

13

# Praise for *POWERHOUSE*

"Kristine Lilly and I share sustained careers with teams who have consistently achieved—hers at the World Cup and Olympics and mine at the Super Bowl. While individuals focus on their own peak performance, a championship-caliber team needs high performing teamwork. If you didn't already know why the United States Women's National Soccer Team consistently wins, you will after reading this book."

**—Tom Brady**, *six-time Super Bowl Champion, New England Patriots*

"The best teams don't just happen. They're built deliberately, strategically, and with care. With tactics and stories drawn from Olympic gold medalist Kristine Lilly's legendary 23 years and 354 international appearances with the US Women's National Soccer Team, this book will help you assemble your own 'powerhouse.'"

**—Sheryl Sandberg**, *COO of Facebook; founder of LeanIn.Org and OptionB.Org*

"With engaging anecdotes and timely advice, Kristine Lilly and her coauthors capture how the values of sports, especially teamwork, apply to anyone leading organizations. *Powerhouse* provides a winning game plan from one of our greatest champions."

**—Adam Silver**, *Commissioner of the National Basketball Association (NBA)*

"*Powerhouse* shows us how teams perform under pressure—whether it is in sports, in business or in life. Kristine Lilly is a superstar on and off the field and she has crafted a strong read on how champions adjust and adapt to build a winning team."

**—Billie Jean King**, *Founder of the Women's Tennis Association, Women's Sports Foundation, and the Billie Jean King Leadership Initiative*

"As a US Army General, I personally experienced the importance of high-performing teamwork during 36 years of service. Whether in Vietnam or Desert Storm, our units, from platoons to much higher headquarters, needed to execute. Lilly and Gillis capture timeless teamwork tactics that will accelerate any team towards success! While on a non-profit board, I worked with Dr. John Gillis, Jr. on strategy development. This is a critical teamwork tactic needed to flourish in the business world, and *Powerhouse* captures many more. This is a must-read this year—by each and every person who is on a team."

**—General James T. Hill**, *United Stated Army (Ret.)*

"In business as in sports, it is thrilling to beat the competition through superior thinking and execution. Kristine Lilly draws on her remarkable history of winning at the highest level of world sport to distill the critical lessons for team formation and performance as the basis of enduring success."

**—Dr. Gary W. Loveman**, *former Chairman and CEO, Caesars Entertainment; Senior Lecturer in Finance, Graduate School of Business, Harvard University*

"Research by the Center for Creative Leadership confirms the critical importance of teamwork and collaboration in driving performance—and the memorable stories in this book show us how to bring these skills to life. In exploring the links between leadership and world-class soccer, the authors inspire us to put their insights to use right away with our own teams."

**—John R. Ryan**, *President and CEO, Center for Creative Leadership*

"Our Olympic gold medalist Women's National Basketball team knows the teamwork tactics that the Women's National Soccer team demonstrates in *Powerhouse*. The lessons in this book will help your team reach its high performing potential. Lilly and Gillis stretch your understanding of what effective teamwork really means and provide an actionable guide on how you can turn your teamwork possibilities into gold medal winning probabilities!"

**—Geno Auriemma**, *United States Women's National Basketball Team Coach, winner of World Championships (2010, 2014) and Olympic Gold medals (2012, 2016)*

"Teams are essential for business success, but they contain tension. How can a leader foster individuals' talents and engagement while simultaneously directing their potentially divergent trajectories toward a shared goal? Lilly, Gillis, and Gillis build from the compelling case of a gold medal sports team that accomplished this integration of individual and group, and they spell out concrete tactics for building similar teams in your organization."

**—Dr. Stanton Wortham**, *Donovan Dean, Lynch School of Education, Boston College*

"When I was CEO, our team grew Calvin Klein's global retail sales from $2.8 to $7.7 billion in ten years. The workplace is not a place for mediocrity or settling. You need team members showing up every day to win, to do their best, to succeed, and to come out ahead. When team members find 'A Great Fit,' they find a place where they belong, where their talents are both fully expressed and needed, and where they can serve the greatest number of people. Lilly, Gillis, and Gillis capture timeless principles that will accelerate any team towards success!"

**—Tom Murry**, *former CEO, Calvin Klein; author, A Great Fit*

"When Kristine Lilly played at North Carolina, her coach Anson Dorrance called her the fire chief, because wherever there was a trouble spot on the field, he could put Kristine and she would put out the fire. It takes great leadership skills to do that at any age, and she shares her insight and techniques to accomplish that in *Powerhouse*."

**—Mack Brown**, *National Champion collegiate football coach*

# POWERHOUSE

## — 13 —

## Teamwork Tactics
## that Build Excellence
## and Unrivaled Success

*Olympic Gold Medalist
and World Cup Champion*
## KRISTINE LILLY *and* DR. JOHN GILLIS, JR.

### with Dr. Lynette Gillis

GREENLEAF
BOOK GROUP PRESS

Published by Greenleaf Book Group Press
Austin, Texas
www.gbgpress.com

Distributed by Greenleaf Book Group

For ordering information or special discounts for bulk purchases, please contact Greenleaf Book Group at PO Box 91869, Austin, TX 78709, 512.891.6100.

Design and composition by Greenleaf Book Group
Cover design by Greenleaf Book Group

Publisher's Cataloging-in-Publication data is available.

Print ISBN: 978-1-62634-638-3

eBook ISBN: 978-1-62634-639-0

Part of the Tree Neutral® program, which offsets the number of trees consumed in the production and printing of this book by taking proactive steps, such as planting trees in direct proportion to the number of trees used: www.treeneutral.com

Printed in the United States of America on acid-free paper

19 20 21 22 23 24 25    10 9 8 7 6 5 4 3 2 1

First Edition

*Kristine's team after they won the 1999 World Cup at the Rose Bowl. She was "So proud to be part of this team!" The coaches from left to right Assistant Coach Lauren Greg, Head Coach Tony Dicicco, and Assistant Coach Jay Hoffman. (Credit: Michael Pimentel/isiphotos.com)*

This book is dedicated to Kristine Lilly's teammates,
and in memory of Coach Tony DiCicco who inspired
many with his constant saying, "I love my job!"

# Contents

## Pillar 1: Transform

## Pillar 2: Empower

## Pillar 3: Achieve

## Pillar 4: Motivate

*Kristine celebrates Olympic gold with her teammate Mia Hamm after their 2–1 overtime victory against Brazil in the final of the 2004 Olympics. Kristine said, "This is one of my favorite photos and wins." (Credit: Michael Pimentel/isiphotos.com)*

# Foreword

**M**y greatest honor as a player was representing my country on our national women's soccer team. Kristine Lilly and I shared that honor over two hundred and fifty times! Wearing the USA uniform brought me some of the best and most memorable moments of my life: the highest of highs and some gut-wrenching losses, but more importantly it has connected me with some of the most extraordinary people. I feel so fortunate to have been a part of such a special group of women who believed it was our responsibility to help grow the game.

I have had so many incredible teammates, all of whom have left their mark on me and helped me be a better player and person. But, it is safe for me to say that there is no one that I would rather line up alongside than Kristine. Kristine was and still is the ultimate teammate. Her work ethic and determination is unmatched. Her attention to detail and fulfillment to the task at hand was legendary. Combine these traits with Kristine's amazing skills, her tireless commitment to the physical and tactical side of the game, as well as her strong mental toughness, and you have one of the best, most consistent players to have ever played soccer. If you needed a player to score an important goal, you could look to Kristine. If you needed a teammate to mark the opposition's best player out of the game, Kristine was your choice. And if you needed a player with the tactical understanding of where to be on a corner kick to save the World Cup for your team by heading a ball off the line, well history can tell you all about that.

I am fortunate to have literally grown up next to one of the greatest players of all time. We came to North Carolina together as freshmen; two young girls from small towns with an entire career ahead of us. Nearly seventeen years later, we had accomplished everything a soccer player could dream of in the form of two World Championships, two Olympic gold medals, and four NCAA titles.

When I take the time to think about it all, it was less about the winning and more about the relationships we built over all of those years and the lessons we learned along the way that have had the greatest impact—like understanding what it meant to show up to practice and to truly invest in the "us" while improving and strengthening the "me." I can still hear Carla Overbeck's voice as we stood on the line for one of our grueling fitness tests in a Florida training camp prior to the 1996 Olympics. She screamed out, "No other team is doing this right now. No one else wants to pay this price to be the best." In this one emotional expression, Carla was challenging us to set a higher standard, empowering us in that we would make every sprint, and supporting us in that we were in this together. I truly believe it was moments like these that forged our team strength and our unconditional belief in each other. Those strong relationships and subsequent winning were based on a strong foundation—a foundation of trust and teamwork.

So when I heard that Kristine was writing a book about her experiences and the importance of teamwork, I was excited to participate and celebrate our team and its historical importance. Many people want to talk about Michelle Akers's greatness, Kristine's incredible skill, Carla and Julie's leadership abilities, but the truth is that we built a foundation for incredible teams. A culture of teamwork that we valued, nurtured, and celebrated. We never took for granted the significance of hard work, selflessness, trust, collaboration, and belief in each other. We forged an understanding that we all had elements of substance to contribute and that every single player was valuable in reaching our goal. This culture enabled us to build successful teams and led us to experience incredible journeys as we prepared and competed for the ultimate prizes in soccer.

Of course, the influence of teamwork transcends the field or playing surface and applies to everything we do in life. Our families and our work life all benefit from these critical beliefs and traits. The most challenging aspect is the consistent commitment it takes to our craft, our job, and our family. I have learned that the most extraordinary people/teams are the ones that commit themselves every day to improve themselves and those around them. They are not as interested in who gets the credit as they are in the group, company, or family experiencing success.

The lessons and stories you will read in the book are from many of the smartest, toughest, and kindest people in the game of soccer. I am so grateful to call so many of them my teammates, and I continue to learn from them now as I did as a player each and every day I put on my cleats or showed up to "work." You have to practice teamwork every single day, just like you practice technical and tactical skills. Our team cared for and loved each other, and we grew from what we experienced together.

**—Mia Hamm**
United States Women's National Soccer Team (1987–2004)
National Soccer Hall of Fame inductee (2007)

# Preface

Through LeadershipX, I have traveled the world helping business executives develop their organizations. In these journeys, I have often seen many individuals not collaborating effectively in assigned work teams. As the amount of workplace teamwork has increased significantly, these low-performing teams negatively impact business performance. I believe that executives could improve teams' performance at their companies if they knew how to focus those teams' skills.

When I began researching this book, I wanted to understand what strategies the most successful teams had in common, as these would drive better financial performance. I also looked for successful sports teams to model, as my reasoning was that if there was a particular team that stood out among all the others, perhaps they could serve as a model for professional organizations, too. The insights from high-performing sports teams could shape the winning tactics that companies need to implement in order to improve their business performance.

There are many great sports teams, from New Zealand's All Blacks rugby team, to the University of Connecticut's Huskies women's basketball team. And the US Women's National Soccer Team just may be the most successful team of all time. On a global stage, they have won three Women's World Cup titles and four Olympic gold medals. According to the Boston Consulting Group, the USWNT was "more successful for a longer period than any team in any other sport." If there was a model for excellence in teamwork, this team was it. I was curious to figure out how they excelled and sustained that excellence for so long.

As fate would have it, I wouldn't have to look far. When my daughter Mary Claire came home from her first day of kindergarten, she told my wife Lynette and me about meeting a new friend, Sidney, on the monkey bars. This playground friendship blossomed. Because Sidney had just moved to Austin, Mary Claire invited her to play on the soccer team that I coached. My coaching qualifications were humble: I'd played soccer all the way to sixth grade before switching to football and moving to the sideline as a male cheerleader in high school, undergraduate, and graduate school. For the five-year-old soccer team, I cheered more than I coached.

You can imagine how surprised I was when I learned that Sidney's mother was *Kristine Lilly*! I was "coaching" the child of one of the world's greatest soccer players.

Thankfully, Kristine proved to be an amazing person, and we grew into family friends. Through our wonderful friendship I learned a lot about how driven she had always been. Kristine is a person who dreams big and works hard until she achieves her goals.

Kristine later told Lynette and me how when she was young she wanted to be in the Olympics. Even then, Kristine believed this dream was fully possible. That is how children dream, with complete conviction. What she didn't know was how much others, the teams in her life, would help her live out her dreams.

As she grew up, Kristine found out how much she loved being on a team. As she joined different sports groups, she loved the friendships that developed from being with other kids, competing together, working toward shared goals, and celebrating. She felt most comfortable on a soccer field. It was the place where she felt at home and free. It was the one place where all things made sense. It was the one place she felt connected. And it became the one place where she would grow as a person and fulfill her dream (goal).

When Kristine was sixteen years old, she was asked by Anson Dorrance to join the US Women's National Soccer Team. Over the course of training, Kristine became close friends with her teammates, and they worked to become one of the most successful teams in US sports history. Her young dream of wanting to be in the Olympics came to fruition when she was twenty-five years old, when she went to Atlanta with Team USA in 1996.

The people who achieved this goal with Kristine made it more than a mere achievement; they made it special. For the first time, Kristine was finally on a team with women whose love for the game mirrored her own. She would remain on the USWNT for the next twenty-three years, and she would go to the Olympics two more times and five World Cups. Throughout all of these amazing achievements, the faces of Kristine's team would change, but at their core, the players that were a part of the world championship teams and gold-medal teams were strikingly similar. All of these women were strong, like-minded athletes who worked hard, pushed each other, did their jobs, communicated, trusted and respected each other, worked together, and loved each other. In order words, they "played for each other."

Throughout this book, you will meet some of these women who wore the USA jersey and impacted Kristine's life, who are world champions and Olympic gold medalists, who know what it means to be part of a team and be successful, and who gave everything they had for the love of the team and the game.

Doesn't that sound like a fantastic high-performing team to glean successful teamwork tactics from?

I asked Kristine to help me understand why the USWNT was so successful for so long. As she outlined these tactics, Lynette and I researched effective teamwork in business. Thus, it should come as no surprise that it also took a team to write this book: Kristine, who shares stories from her Women's National Soccer Team experiences; Lynette, who provides research from her university leadership; and me, who contributes my business experiences from my work in management consulting.

In the pages ahead, you will learn how to cultivate well-oiled teamwork in your own organization. I'm not going to kid you and say that it will always be easy, but with practice and perseverance, you will be well on your way to building your own powerhouses. As Kristine says, "Always believe!"

—**Dr. John Gillis, Jr.**
Founder, LeadershipX

*Kristine celebrates after scoring against England in the quarterfinals of the 2007 World Cup. It was her only goal of the tournament, and it was her last goal in a World Cup. The team won 3–0 that day. (Credit: Trent Davol/isiphotos.com)*

# Introduction

*"Wearing the same jersey does not make a team."*

**—Author Unknown**

High-performing teams are more effective than a collection of high-performing individuals. They create value and impact. In the business world, these high-performing groups are called "A teams," and they are increasingly important as corporations seek higher quality work, shorter amounts of time to complete a task, and superior outputs.

Henry Ford, famous for assembling cars with a production line, once said, "Coming together is a beginning. Keeping together is progress. Working together is success."[1] Each member on high-performing teams trusts the others and feels accountable for the team's success. These workers tend to have higher senses of satisfaction because they know they are making a difference for their colleagues and organization.

The basic idea behind any team is that this group of individuals can achieve superior results when compared to a group of individuals working side by side.

---

1    Erika Andersen, "Quotes from Henry Ford on Business Leadership," Forbes.com, May 31, 2013, https://www.forbes.com/sites/erikaandersen/2013/05/31/21-quotes-from-henry-ford-on-business-leadership-and-life/#225a3c59293c.

## Not All Groups Are Teams

Do all groups achieve superior outcomes? While the name "team" is generously given to a group of people, for many it is TINO (Team in Name Only) or a convening group of people.

For many people, working on teams can be frustrating. They can feel like the "team" is hindering the individual's progress or that involving more colleagues in a project only results in an increase of tedious meetings. Successful teams are the result of effort, leadership, and an enabling attitude. Without these, a mere collection of people following orders creates less than desirable results. If anyone is at odds with the team objective, the fabric of the teamwork will fray. The relationships between team members can become strained, leading to mistrust, conflict, and disagreement that hinder the job from being completed effectively.

As a result, many businesses consider teams to be a necessary evil but fail to appreciate them. Later, their skepticism appears to be proved right when teams underperform and do not live up to their expectations. Surprisingly, most organizations do not dedicate the time and/or resources that are needed to fully develop their teams. Patrick Lencioni wrote in *The Five Dysfunctions of a Team*, "It is teamwork that remains the ultimate competitive advantage, both because it is so powerful and so rare." To unlock this competitive advantage and avoid TINOs in your organization, you can learn from one of the most competitive and successful teams of all time—the USWNT.

## Powerhouse

Teamwork is a vital competency for businesses—and the secret to revolutionizing your organization. Once you and your employees have experienced a high-performing team, you will not want to go back to a TINO.

In the sports world, these desirable, synergistic groups that work together and achieve success are called **powerhouses**. Building a powerhouse takes time and energy, but the end results justify this effort.

> **Powerhouse**
> (noun) [paủ(-ə)r-haủs]:
> A team having great energy, strength, and potential for success.

When it comes to building a powerhouse, it would be hard to find someone who has a more impressive resume than Kristine Lilly. She played in 354 games, the most out of anyone in the game of soccer, male or female, during her over twenty-three years on the USWNT. Yet, not only her duration sets her apart, but also the fact that these were all high-performing teams, playing in five World Cups (1991, 1995, 1999, 2003, 2007) and three Olympics (1996, 2000, 2004), where they won two gold medals and two world championships!

As a midfielder, she was the collaborator between the offense and the defense, the communicator who drove team execution, the team member who played longer than any other player. She truly was the ideal person to understand high-performing teams, due to her longevity at the highest level and her role on the field.

According to Kristine, the USWNT team never thought of themselves as a powerhouse. She says, "We believed we were the best, but we knew we had to prove it every time we stepped on the field. We built our team with constant hard work—and humility—that sustained excellence over decades. Our unrivaled success was a result of these thirteen teamwork tactics." Unbeknownst to them, their hard work, relentless energy, strength, and success define them as a powerhouse.

We've grouped chapters into four actions that teams need to take. These pillars are: **T**ransform, **E**mpower, **A**chieve, and **M**otivate. The final tactic, "Doing What Is Right," serves as a foundation for everything the team accomplishes. As a team takes these four actions, they are closer to building their powerhouse, which will be described as a distinguishable group of selected competent people with diverse talents and experiences who complete a shared objective that cannot be achieved by individuals alone.

## Transform

Effectively transforming a group of individuals into a powerhouse starts with selecting the right talent to join your team. This team determines their purpose as well as their strategy. Once a strategy is set for execution, each team member acts interdependently to contribute to the completion of a clear, specified, and common goal.

## Empower

To empower a powerhouse, there is a leader who inspires, sets expectations, and develops others individually and collectively. Principled leadership asserts authority in an empowering manner, aligning individual rewards with the team's goals. If the situation is global, there is an opportunity to cross-pollinate better practices from different countries as well as building cultural awareness while working virtually.

## Achieve

To achieve, the powerhouse must learn through preparation, practicing, and then the actual performance. The people who make up the team collaborate through honest communication and listen to each other so that each decision is made cooperatively. When a problem does emerge, the team engages together to generate, evaluate, and implement a proactive or reactive solution. Their resilience enables them to bounce back.

## Motivate

The members of a powerhouse create a team culture, based on trust, with specific roles clarified for each person. Through the work that the members of the team are committed to, they build friendships and a sense of belonging together as well as their own individual self-awareness. They have a positive mentality while seeking a standard of excellence for their team deliverable. When a high-performing team acts synergistically, each team member receives great satisfaction.

Most importantly, all team members do the right thing, as they overcome adversity with a diverse team acting ethically.

# Thirteen Teamwork Tactics for Your Business

On the field, Kristine was a master at dictating the game and setting up her teammates for success. The teams that Kristine played with were critical to her unparalleled success as an athlete. But, the individual accolades and experiences she had would not have been possible without the efforts of her teammates.

In the pages ahead, you will learn more about how she and her teammates successfully and continuously won World Cup championships and Olympic gold medals, and how you can apply these same "tactics" to shape your business's journey forward to success. Complementing Kristine and her teammates' expertise, you'll find research on teamwork and business examples from John and Lynette Gillis. As a management consultant, John has worked with many organizations and observed their good as well as poor teamwork. When he facilitates the Leadership Xperience business simulation, it is quickly apparent which teams are high performing and which teams will crater under the pressure of executing a business strategy. To complement Kristine's powerhouse experience, he has leveraged his corporate experience with evidence-based findings on the tactics that make teams successful. As you read, you will learn how you can develop teamwork skills within yourself and your employees to improve your company's performance.

As a tribute to Kristine's jersey number, we have created a thirteen-chapter structure for this book, each exploring a key tactic that will help you unlock your teams' potential.

## A Note about Lucky 13

The #13 jersey has been worn by many famous professional athletes like the National Basketball Association's (NBA) Wilt Chamberlain, who scored 100 points in one game for the Philadelphia 76ers. Lindsay Whalen, who was the University of Minnesota's all-time leading scorer before joining the Lynx in the Women's National Basketball Association's (WNBA), also wore the jersey. In Major League Baseball (MLB), Alex Rodriguez sported #13 when he was MVP while hitting home runs for the Yankees. Even the National Football League's (NFL) Kurt Warner, who went from undrafted to MVP when he won the Super Bowl with the Rams, wore #13, and the National Hockey League (NHL)'s Pavel Datsyuk won multiple Stanley Cups and the Selkes and Lady Byngs awards with the seemingly lucky #13 on his back. With all of these successful athletes wearing #13, why would anyone think this number is unlucky?

*continued*

Kristine Lilly's raw talent and incredible team aptitude prompts people to want #13, starting a new tradition in soccer today. The current US Women's National Soccer Team's co-captain Alex Morgan wears #13 too, continuing the number's tradition of excellence. When asked about her jersey number, Alex said:

*"When I watched Kristine Lilly play in the 1999 World Cup, I was inspired. She represented the national team, and I looked up to her while I was growing up. I wanted to one day wear #13 like her.*

*"I had the chance to play with my role model Kristine for six months when our USWNT careers overlapped. She was a like a big sister to me and a large part of our team.*

*"When Lil retired in 2011, she passed the number 13 down to me, and I appreciated that immensely and have worn it with pride ever since. It's not a common number for a soccer player, yet I believe that many young players today are gravitating to #13 because of Kristine's legacy. Lil represented #13 on the high stage, and these kids, like me, are determined to follow her footsteps. Lucky 13!"*

Each chapter begins with compelling stories from the field that show you the real-life application of the tactic in play, and then progresses into an informative look at how you can apply the corresponding powerhouse principle. We'll get to speak with some of Kristine's teammates who share their own reflections on teamwork and how it helped them achieve powerhouse experiences both on and off the field.

By the time you complete this book, you will be well on your way to building your own powerhouse winning team.

## Pillar 1:

# TRANSFORM

To build a powerhouse, you first need to transform the group of selected individuals into team members. To thoroughly change the character of this group into the appearance of a team and not a TINO, you need these team members to align to a team direction. This team will then work together to achieve their goals. These initial essential tactics are critical to team formation, but many teams forget to focus on these fundamentals, failing to transform. When you effectively transform, a group of individual contributors becomes a high-performing powerhouse.

*Brandi Chastain celebrates after scoring the penalty kick to win the 1999 World Cup in the Rose Bowl on July 10th. "This is one of the most expressive and emotional photos," Kristine said. "It still fills me with so much emotion." (Credit: Barnimir Kvartuc/ZUMAPRESS/isiphotos.com)*

# Selecting Exceptional Team Members

*"Each team has their own character, and you must be willing to accept team member differences. It's important to accept each person's uniqueness, while embracing the ultimate objective and goal of the team."*

—**Brandi Chastain**

When Kristine was only sixteen years old and a junior in high school, she was asked to join the US Women's National Soccer Team (USWNT), which changed her life. She not only would also be a part of arguably one of the most successful sports teams ever, but she would join forces with individuals who would accept and support one another to be the best.

During her first trip with the USWNT, to China, Kristine scored the first goal of her international career, and she became the youngest player to ever score a goal for the national team. This trip began Lilly's journey with the USWNT that would last over two and a half decades, including over three hundred games and over three hundred thousand minutes of game time. Just before her retirement in 2011, Kristine became the oldest player to ever score for the USWNT. As of 2018, she still holds the record for both the youngest and oldest player to score a goal for the USWNT.[2] This incredible feat illustrates that Lilly's remarkable skill never diminished, or as Kristine said at her US Soccer Hall of Fame (HOF) induction in 2015, "Scoring your first goal makes you feel like you belong. Scoring your last goal makes you feel like you still belong."

Kristine's exceptional play in high school and then on her regional team captured the attention of the US Women's National Team coach, Anson Dorrance. Anson asked her, Mia Hamm, Linda Hamilton, Julie Foudy, and Joy Fawcett to join the USWNT. These young players would join forces for seventeen years and understand what it means to be part of a team. Mia Hamm, who also became Kristine's teammate at the University of North Carolina in 1989, summed up what it means to be a on a winning team, "I was a member of a team, and I relied on the team. I defer to it and sacrifice for it, because the team, not the individual, is the ultimate champion." For these young players, knowing only the most exceptional athletes from all over the country would come together gave them the drive, connection, and respect for the teams they created together.

## Why Selection Is Important

A team's effectiveness is dependent on its collective and complementary team member skills. For businesses, attracting, hiring, and retaining high-quality employees is an ongoing focus. Talent acquisition can be an arduous and high-pressure process: companies must create employee value propositions to attract key prospects, identifying future employees who will "fit" with organizational culture and contribute, and the stakes are high. Beyond the significant cost-per-hire, a wrong hire can threaten further damage to teams.

To create a powerhouse on the field or in the boardroom, the first tactic you need to learn is how to select team members effectively. You need to identify high-potential individuals, recruit to build or buy talent, and go for green and gray.

---

2    "U.S. Soccer Legend Kristine Lilly Retires," USsoccer.com, January 5, 2011, https://www.ussoccer.com/stories/2014/03/17/12/57/us-soccer-legend-kristine-lilly-retires.

# Build High-Potential Individuals

In 1986, Kristine didn't know that there was a US Women's National Soccer Team. The USWNT had just played its inaugural match a year prior under the direction of Coach Mike Ryan in Jesolo, Italy. The game was by all accounts not very memorable, as the USA lost to Italy 1–0.[3]

Coach Anson Dorrance had been hired to take over from Ryan, and he was determined to replace the founding team's collection of largely unknown players with strong, indelible athletes. Coach Dorrance was known for his skill for identifying talent for his team at The University of North Carolina. Each was a player with high potential who brought strengths to the team. These young women, in regional play, had already demonstrated an internal drive and a desire to learn and grow. Dorrance envisioned future roles for them, seeking potential to develop and establish the foundation for the USWNT for years to come.

## Value Potential

In order to correctly identify high potentials, Dorrance had to select players based more on the person's technical and tactical skills instead of their physical characteristics, such as height and strength. Kristine and Mia, being five foot four and five foot five, respectively, did not mean that they had less talent than a player nearly six feet tall like Michelle Akers, and Dorrance knew to value their quick thinking and speed. As research of soccer player selection in Switzerland showed, it can be challenging for many coaches to think long term in regard to their players; there is immediate pressure on short-term success in sport.[4] However, in soccer and in business, a long-term and process-oriented approach to recruitment will result in better results at the top levels. High-potential individuals selected for their long-term impact on the team rather than short-term wins can lead to a reputation for high quality as well as a sustainable achievement record.

In the business world, talent acquisition mirrors the struggle for assembling winning teams in soccer. Employers may overlook an applicant with a high potential to benefit the organization in the long term, instead hiring based

---

3    "32 Years of USWNT Glory," FIFA.com, August 18, 2017, https://www.fifa.com/womens-football/news/32-years-of-uswnt-glory-2904417.

4    Michael Romann and Jörg Fuchslocher, "Influence of the Selection Level, Age and Playing Position on Relative Age Effects in Swiss Women's Soccer," *Talent Development & Excellence* 3, no. 2 (October 2011): 239–47.

on immediate need and short-term pressure. To effectively hire for potential, a company needs to not only assess an applicant's skill and experiences—what a resume details—but also assess for potential, which is harder to ascertain. Talent acquisition professionals use employee referrals, psychometric assessments, references, and other background measures to try and identify this "black box." When a leader forsakes a process-oriented and organic employee development approach, they are effectively deciding that they don't want to "build" or develop a candidate's potential over time. This potential is more valuable for your organization to identify for long-term performance. Winning today—on the field and in business—is important; yet, building a team to win at the elite levels tomorrow requires hiring for potential now.

## A Note about Bad Hires

Everybody, even professional recruiters and coaches, makes mistakes from time to time. However, if you've come to realize that one of your new team members is not a good choice, you should act swiftly.

Hiring or recruiting a person to your team who is not aligned to your values can have a negative effect on other team members' morale and confidence. Bad hires have a ripple effect throughout the organization, dragging overall team performance down. The wrong person keeping a chair warm doesn't only underperform in their role; they make high-potential teammates resentful, increase conflict, and can even lead to turnover. If you determine that you've made a bad hire, it's better to terminate the wrong hire immediately and rehire to find the right fit for your team, than to try to force a bad hire to work out. As a smart colleague of mine once said, "If an employee or team member isn't right, you should free up their future." By removing them from your team, not only do you preserve your team's integrity and open up the possibility for a good recruit to replace them, you also give the "bad" hire the opportunity to find a place where they fit and succeed.

If you don't, you are deciding that you don't care about winning anytime soon: victory is significantly delayed when a bad hire gets to stick around.

# Buy Talent

While the tactic of hiring high potentials leads to organic career development growth over time, most companies still find themselves with capability gaps that must be addressed immediately by acquiring experienced hires. If building talent isn't quite possible on your schedule, your other option is to "buy" a new team member in the competitive war for talent.

In addition to being a sport, professional soccer is a business. Better field performance leads to higher revenue. The more money that comes to a team from winning, the more teams can in turn increase their wages and "buy" quality talent. This investment in talent then leads to even better field performance.

To learn about buying talent, let's look at Manchester United (ManU), one of the most financially successful professional male soccer teams.[5] When the Premier League was founded in 1992, this club won four of the first six annual titles and got second place the other two years. Even today, they dominate the soccer merchandise market and sell match tickets at premium prices despite being in a crowded market with twenty other teams because their brand is one of the strongest. As their team won over the past decades, revenues grew. The financial outcomes of millions in profits are healthy for any company. However, in the professional soccer industry where most clubs report a pretax loss, their results are staggering.

In the English football Premier League, unlike baseball, basketball, or American football, the organization does not attempt to provide parity between teams and balance the competition by redistributing income, installing a maximum wage, or controlling player transfers. Successful teams must spend money to acquire talent and continuously harvest their profits to buy talent in order to preserve their competitiveness on the field. The quality of the team increases the amount of revenues that allow teams to acquire highly talented players, resulting in improved performances on the field. So, when we talk about ManU's success when the Premier League was founded, the story actually started three years earlier. That summer, ManU went on a spending spree to buy talent with five key experienced players: Gary Pallister, Neil Webb, Paul Ince, Mike Phelan, and Danny Wallace. For ManU, these talented players built their teamwork over three years and established a reputation for winning and a

5    Stefan Szymanski, "Why Is Manchester United So Successful?" *Business Strategy Review 9*, no. 4 (December 1998): 47–54.

loyal fan base in a crowded and competitive marketplace. These are the players that set the foundation that would propel them to a winning culture for the next several decades.

## Compete with A-Team Talent

How can you ensure that your company will thrive in a competitive environment like ManU? Your business will compete against similar organizations for revenue, profitability, and clients. Having A-Team talent can help you win against your competitors.

The need for agility and competitiveness underscores your company's need to hire high-potential individuals, future stars, in order to succeed against your competitors, but sometimes your organization may not have the ability to wait for your recruits to develop their potential. In these situations, you can take a play from ManU and buy talent for an immediate, short-term impact on your organization.

We do mean "buy" quite literally. C-Team players are readily available at cheap prices; however, A-Team players typically require higher salaries, bigger sign-on bonuses, and attractive benefits packages. You'll need to invest financially in them in order to recruit them effectively. A-Team employees can also be harder to find, especially because they tend to be already employed by other organizations who are trying hard to retain them. However, if you decide to use this strategy and make the investment to attract one of these A-Team individuals, you hopefully will end up removing a lot of the uncertainty and time that "building" players can involve. Ideally your investment will contribute to a solid team that consistently generates more revenue for you. In turn, this will help you to buy more high-level talent to keep your business successful in the short term while you build your high-potential individuals to improve your company's long-term performance.

## Go Green and Gray

When Kristine was a freshman at UNC, members of the soccer team had a fitness test to run 7 ¼ laps in 12 minutes, or else they could not play in a game. Their fitness test was not loved, but it was a benchmark hopefuls needed to pass to be on the team. The test measured the player's fitness levels, but it also built respect and trust among the team. With a lap to go, as a "green" inexperienced player, Kristine was really struggling. Tracey Bates Leone, a "gray" senior on the team, decided to help by running backward next to Kristine and encouraging her, even though this meant Tracey would have a slower finish time on the fitness test that she, too, had to pass. Both were able to pull each other through and finish the lap on time.

Kristine and Tracey would also be teammates on the USWNT. Kristine, still green, eventually ended up earning the starting role over the same gray player, Tracey Bates Leone, who had helped her pass her fitness test at UNC. Tracey did not complain, nor did she hold it against Kristine. Instead, she helped her teammate.

Coach Dorrance later overheard Tracey talking to her mother on the phone after Kristine unseated her. Tracey said, "Don't you understand, Kristine is better than I am."[6] Tracey understood the greening and graying team process of hiring younger, less experienced players to work with the older players with more experience.

Many workforces are a combination of green, gray, and those in between. Not only does each generation bring various levels of experience, they also tend to have different working styles. For companies to be successful, they must learn how to effectively develop and execute with both green and gray team members collaborating for performance.

Coach Dorrance understood the need to retain "gray" players and use their experience to help push the USWNT to ever greater levels. Kristine, after some time on the team, became a "gray" who mentored the players selected after her. Before her retirement in 2011, Kristine had to earn her position every year for twenty-three consecutive years to be able to stay on the team, and during that time she had many opportunities to help train and develop the potential in others. As a member of the National Team, everyone went through the process of being "green," and somewhere along the way someone helped them. Kristine always reached out to these new players, sometimes in small ways, to assist when they had their first games with the national team. One player was Heather O'Reilly, who was playing in her first game. After a couple of runs on the field, Kristine sensed Heather's nervousness through her heavy breathing.

6   Peter Tollman, Josh Serlin, Michelle Akers, Anson Dorrance, "The Power of Inspiration, Perspiration, and Cooperation—in Sports and in Business," The Boston Consulting Group, June 13, 2018, https://www.bcg.com/publications/2018/power-inspiration-perspiration-cooperation-sports-business.aspx.

The simple words "Heather, relax, you will do great" helped Heather tremendously to have support from a veteran player.

Kristine was the first woman to play in five different World Cups, winning consistently and never finishing less than third place. In soccer, instead of saying "international games played," they use "caps." This historical and now metaphorical term is from when the United Kingdom gave an actual cap for your head to every player. Kristine's 354 caps surpassed Norway's Heidi Støre's, the previous women's world record holder of 151 caps, and the United Arab Emirates' Adnan Al-Talyani, who held the men's world record at 164 caps. Twenty-three years later, after all those games, marriage, and the birth of her first daughter (which is why she missed the 2008 Olympics) . . . she was "graying." If Coach Dorrance had only thought of training in terms of "green," he would have missed out on the complementary benefits of the "gray" that Kristine and others brought to the team.

## Develop Strong Multigenerational Teams

Team composition contributes to a team's efficiency. If you have a collection of diverse team members, a heterogeneous group, your team will be stronger and more effective. At your corporation, your team members will come from a continuum of "green" and "gray" colleagues. These different generations bring different skills, experiences, expectations, and other factors to the workplace. As you build successful teams, the key is to not only identify, yet also optimize each person's unique and diverse offerings for the benefit of the unit.

Teamwork requires diverse, cross-boundary abilities, which are greater than what a single individual can contribute. These complementary abilities and range of specialized expertise that come from mixing professionals at different stages of their careers enable the team members to learn from each other and make the team highly productive. Green hires can help graying colleagues understand emerging technologies or introduce new ideas to the discussion, and their more senior colleagues can share hard-won lessons from their experiences.

As a leader, you can identify the team's gaps and coordinate the shape of the group so that team members complement each other and the team is not critically exposed. Each team member has strengths that you can capitalize on, as well as areas needing improvements that you know to avoid when performance is critical. For example, at the Federal Reserve Bank, outside each team member's cubicle is their name as well as their strengths and communication preferences. This simple posting near the individual's name helps team members learn how to most effectively work with one another. This improved working relationship increases the team's capacity and production.

These intangibles can seem elusive to correctly identify during the hiring process, but being open to finding talent in places along the experience continuum where you may not have hired from before can greatly enhance your possibility of success.

## Enable Team Stability

Another benefit of incorporating the green and gray tactic is the continuity that graying membership can provide. These team members cultivate security for your team by maintaining set expectations and cohesive team values over the course of their tenure. Leaders often think about how new team members will "fit" with the rest of the team in the short term, yet with the right mix, veterans can ensure new teams and new hires are set up for long-term success. These teams are like a bottle of wine, where all the ingredients are present at the beginning, and time allows them to gradually reach full potential. Team values that were established and reinforced by gray members early on became part of the team's identity, and then, even as gray members may leave the team, formerly green colleagues continue to teach these values. This process provides stability for each subsequent team.

Your business team, even when new members join, should focus on onboarding and assimilation so that you can maintain a sense of stability. Teams need a steady foundation that they can rely on to perform at their best. With this solid foundation in place, team members learn how to best work together, and this only improves over time.

## Invest in Team Continuity

Powerhouses do not happen quickly. Teams mostly develop by the amount of time their members spend working together, talking with one another, and getting to know each other. The synergy of an excellent team comes from strong relationships between colleagues—both professionally as well as personally. These relationships help them read each other and to know how to execute when it comes time to perform. They understand each other's interests, their perspectives, and their daily work process, challenges, and deliverables. There is no substitute for quality time together to learn more about each other.

In order to build a powerhouse, you will need to recruit and develop high-potential individuals, buy talent, and mix the green and gray. Brandi Chastain, most famous for the final penalty kick goal in the 1999 World Cup final, discusses how to apply these principles in the following interview.

# 1:1 with Brandi Chastain

Brandi was a two-time FIFA World Cup champion and a two-time Olympic gold medalist. She was inducted into the National Soccer Hall of Fame in 2017. Brandi cofounded an after-school program for underserved girls in the San Francisco Bay Area that is known as Bay Area Women's Sports Initiative or BAWSI.org.

## How do you effectively bring together high-potential individuals on a team?

When you are in an environment that is hypercompetitive like the USWNT, the standards of excellence are through the roof. It can be overwhelming when you first come into it. My teammates and I grew to embrace it. You have to start in a place you're uncomfortable in order to be better. We were all in. Our team had diversity and conflict, and we grew through resolution and problem solving. Success is not linear; it is messy—you can go up and down and sideways and backward, twisting and turning on the way to your goal.

As a coach, I look for fast, strong, and technical—physical traits that stand out right away. Yet, I also look for the mental skills that you have to be patient to unearth and cultivate. Each team has its own character, and you must be willing to accept team member differences. It's important to accept each person's uniqueness, while embracing the ultimate objective and goal of the larger team. Each person has their own perspective, values, and skills they bring to the table. Your team needs unique personalities and characters, and you can't have everyone be the same. When you have that, then you have confidence and security.

## How was it being on a team with top talent?

Our coach established our common goal, yet he wasn't always the driver of the bus. He was just the mechanic. He knew how the team worked and could fix it when we started breaking down, but it came down to each of us on the team and how we pushed each other to really make sure we were developing to our full potential.

The expectations our team demanded for fitness were very high, above most people. Knowing that, you could feel trepidation, nervousness, and anxiety. Every day mattered. We were working, building, and investing toward that game moment.

Kristine was always a driving force in our fitness; she managed to find a way to push the envelope a little bit more to give a little extra. Work was going to cost you something. Getting over the hurdle wasn't easy. You had to be willing to invest in yourself and in your team. Kristine was inspiring, leading by example. It would have been easy to give up and say, "I can't do one more," especially when you were pushing the maximum effort already. Through Kristine's leadership, our team would rise above any obstacle, because she was willing to invest in those moments. The saying, "I have your back and you have my back" comes to mind. Our team, when led by her in fitness, would always find "just one more."

If you know that kind of teamwork is present, you can do anything.

## Can you give us an example of the green and gray tactic from your experience?

For the USWNT to be successful, we needed to feel involved. We embraced the "green" players who were there, because we knew they had something to contribute. It did not matter if a player was young and goofy or old and cranky, we had a common goal: to be the best and win. Veterans had all been through a first practice, so we would onboard the new players and show them how to do it. We told them, "You are going to be faced with moments when you are out of your comfort zone. When you are faced with change, you have choices. I was given the opportunity to change, and I embraced that change. You can too."

In 1995, when I was left off the USWNT as they added "green" players, I was disappointed and sad. Being away from the team and missing the World Cup was really difficult. However, when Coach DiCicco invited me back onto the team in 1996 as a "gray" member, I had the support of the players and coach. I was really excited to head back to that environment and do what I loved.

Then I got the bombshell that I was not returning to play in a forward position, as I had for most of my career. Instead, I was being asked to play as a defender. In that moment, I had a choice. I could have too much pride and say I wanted to be a forward and be valued in that way, or, I could say this is an amazing opportunity to get out of my comfort zone and challenge myself. I chose the second option, as there was a great team supporting me, and if the coach didn't believe in me and my ability to play as a strong defender, he wouldn't have put me back on the team. Rather than seeing it as a negative, of "forced" into playing a position I didn't want to be, I had a "hey, go for it" mentality.

As I learned my new position, I brought many of the skills I'd developed playing forward. We changed the defense position to be more attacking— and this started a sport-wide trend that continues today. Instead of being a man-marker that destroys opponents, our outside backs now play like attacking wingers. I was momentarily upset about my position being changed, but instead I was part of revolutionizing the defense position! Looking back, I am really satisfied. It was not what I thought it would be like, yet I did it being open, honest, and agile. I did not lose the power of the moments during the journey; I was present.

## Tactics for Your Team

When selecting team members, it's important to hire high-potential individuals so you build your talent pipeline with candidates who are future stars. You also want to buy talent to improve business performance immediately, which enables you to continue to acquire and retain top talent to improve corporate/financial performance. As you're incorporating new members, try to mix together "green" and "gray" teammates to create optimal team environments that are full of diverse people with complementary skill sets.

Consider applying these three principles to your own organization. How will you:

**1.** Select high-potential new hires who will drive business in the future?

**2.** Actively seek "A-Team" mature talent to enhance team performance?

**3.** Incorporate diverse experience and complementary expertise to optimize the team?

*"Walking out onto the field as a team before the whistle always filled me with nerves and a sense of honor,"* Kristine said. This picture was taken at Giant Stadium, where the women played a friendly game on June 23, 2007, against Brazil, which ended in a 2–0 win for the USA. (Credit: John Todd/isiphotos.com)

# Aligning the Team Direction

*"When you give decisions to the team to make, this*
*increases team participation, responsibility, and accountability,*
*and it's very strengthening to the team."*

—**Marissa Mayer**

The journey of women's professional soccer isn't much different from other men's leagues that started following a journey of ups and downs, of revision and realignment. The Women's United Soccer Association (WUSA) had its inaugural season in 2001 with eight teams, basking in the glory of the unprecedented media coverage of the 1999 Women's World Cup Finals. The players' last and final goal was to have a Women's Professional league.

The WUSA wanted to be the world's premier women's professional soccer league. This desire was its foundational purpose—and this was an ambitious goal, as even the men's professional soccer league had failed three times before it could sustain itself with the American Soccer League (1921–33), the North American Soccer League (1967–84), and ultimately, Major League Soccer (1996–present).

Unfortunately, WUSA's first attempt was not successful. Kristine moved to Boston to start playing for the Boston Breakers in the WUSA. After a long history of men's professional athletics, the women playing in the league were excited to be professional athletes. The best players in America and from around the world were playing in this league. On her team in Boston, Kristine had the two top players from Germany and two from Norway; two rival countries were now her teammates. She recalls, "It was a dream come true to get to do what I loved for a living." Unfortunately, that dream was cut off after three years. The league ran out of funds and folded just before the 2003 World Cup.

A short time later, another new league attempted to revamp women's professional soccer. However, that also ended after three seasons. Then, US Soccer decided to step in and get involved: they began the National Women's Soccer League in 2013, and it is still going strong.

To be successful, a business's revenue must exceed expenses, and this is the same for sports leagues too, as their revenue sources include ticket sales, broadcast rights, sponsorship, and merchandise. Unfortunately, while the WUSA's purpose was sound, the strategy, or direction that the organization took, was flawed. The most glaring problem was that league expenditures far outpaced revenues. The ill-fated WUSA was depending on augmenting their revenue with strategic philanthropy from companies who would support the women's cause. When looking at the league's expenses, they made a commitment to do everything in a "first class" manner. This was great from a public-relations perspective; however, it was fiscally unsustainable.

The WUSA had high overhead for office and stadium rentals as well as high travel fees as teams traveled coast to coast. A quick look at the league's income statement showed that $3.7 million was spent on general expenses, including yearly advertising, corporate sales, sponsor services, and public relations costs. Not only was this high, it was significantly more than they had budgeted. The $7.8 million spent on player salaries and benefits was barely more than the "spare no expense" extravagant league office expenses of $7.2 million.[7]

That was just the league's finances. Each team also had additional expenses, television broadcasts, team operations, advertising and promotion, game day operations, and non-player salaries. These varied between teams; however, the Washington Freedom was the most successful team with the highest attendance, and they even lost roughly $1.3 million.

---

7   Richard M. Southall, Mark S. Nagel, Deborah J. LeGrande, "Build It and They Will Come? The Women's United Soccer Association: A Collision of Exchange Theory and Strategic Philanthropy," *Sport Marketing Quarterly* 14, no. 3 (2005).

As with most start-ups, the league's founders invested in the organization, knowing that it would not be profitable for a while. They expected to lose $15 million during the first three years. Instead, they lost $20 million the first year alone. This total grew to $100 million during the league's three-year existence.

A better direction that the WUSA should have followed is that of the Arena Football League (AFL), a slow-growth league that started with four teams and now has nineteen teams thirty years later. The AFL kept operating expenses low until attendance and exposure increased enough to enable them to upgrade. Even the early NBA and NFL, while successful today, took decades to grow their fan bases. Their expenses were in line and reflective of their slow economic development.

## Why Alignment Is Important

In any business, you must establish purpose and execute a solid strategy to be successful. When problems arise, they must be addressed. An unclear sense of strategy, lack of purpose, and a team not aligned to a common direction for the business to market can quickly create problems. A team needs to align and unify, as a business direction dictates how you are going to sell your product or service to a market to make a profit.

A team's purpose and strategy align the team to a direction, as well as prioritizing tasks to focus on. Both are needed for an organization to win. After that, you need to be able to solve problems effectively. If a company is ineffective in establishing purpose and strategy, as well as solving problems, then they will unfortunately follow a similar path as the WUSA. A team should focus on these three principles.

## Establish Raison d'Être

All successful teams need a reason for being or existence, which is their raison d'être. Organizations that have a meaningful and understood purpose will outperform those that do not. The reason for this is simple: Those organizations have focus and ambition behind their work. Purpose answers the question, "Why do you do what you do?" Purpose drives performance.

The company purpose details your positive impact on the customer whom you are serving. Whether your company purpose is to nourish a family, mitigate their financial risk, buy one/donate one, or something else, the team direction has a clear desired goal answering the question, "why?" This end state will engage and energize the team members. A team can envision the "big picture" future once they know their raison d'être, and then work backward from that end goal to detail the actions they need to take to reach it. Many companies struggle to establish a purpose for their workers, as leaders do not understand how important it is for motivation and aligning efforts. A purpose is more than a tagline; it is a well-articulated guiding light—the North Star—that motivates employees, attracts customers, and provides reason for their team's existence.

Coach Dorrance once told the USWNT that "every time you step on the field you're selling the game, changing minds, and changing the culture of what is possible for women and for everyone."[8] In doing so, he was helping them understand their purpose. When Kristine first heard this statement, her response was, "I just want to play soccer. What does he mean 'sell the game'?" Eventually, she came to understand everything he taught them and each action they took on the field was selling the game. They were helping not only themselves as athletes become more successful but also their team, and by extension they were helping to establish women's soccer as a professional sport. All of this, in turn, reinforced their reason for being and for playing the game.

Dorrance's directions to his players all connected to their larger purpose of establishing themselves as professionals and helping to grow the love of their sport. He wanted them to play with their shirts tucked in and their socks pulled up, as well as to sign autographs after every game for every fan. When they traveled as a team or ate a team meal, they all wore matching outfits. As a result, when they were on the field, they played soccer with passion and love. They played an attacking style that not only advanced their plays up the field but also showed their passion. Above all, they enjoyed themselves, because he had given them purpose.

Coach Dorrance's team loved what they did and did it in a fashion that people loved to watch. As a result, their team embraced Coach Dorrance's higher calling. "It wasn't really for us. It was for the future of women's soccer,"

---

8    Peter Tollman, Josh Serlin, Michelle Akers, Anson Dorrance, "The Power of Inspiration, Perspiration, and Cooperation—in Sports and in Business," The Boston Consulting Group, June 13, 2018, https://www.bcg.com/publications/2018/power-inspiration-perspiration-cooperation-sports-business.aspx.

Captain Carla Overbeck recalled.[9] Another way that Coach Dorrance established this purpose for his players was by teaching them along the way who they were going to be. When he would ask them a question, he would start with, "OK, future coaches of America . . ." He wanted them to think about their destiny while they were playing. He instilled in them the information that would stick in their heads the rest of their lives.

There must be an uplifting and ambitious purpose that resonates with the team. This purpose for your team must inspire team members while they are executing the day-to-day tasks aligned to the strategy.

## Encourage Engagement

For most of your employees, a purpose is not simply financial targets like increased revenues or cutting costs. People need a more compelling incentive than that to get out of bed in the morning. It's not just about success; it's also about significance. As one building supply company CEO shared, employees need a deeper purpose beyond making money to be engaged with their job.

This raison d'être will compel employees to work hard, be engaged, and enjoy their jobs. When each team member understands how their daily tasks directly contribute to the team's long-term objectives, their commitment to the team and engagement with their job increases significantly. This helps team members feel valued, engaged, and involved. These passionate employees bring their whole self to work. Purpose challenges you to persist and excel over time.

Many companies define a mission (what we do), vision (what the company plans to achieve), and values (how we work together) yet fail to embed the purpose (why we do it) into their DNA.

When your employees have relevant and meaningful belief in the value of their work, it will make your business stronger. Purpose aligns and unifies team members toward their collective effort. Andrew Carnegie, late nineteenth-century steel industrialist, said, "Teamwork is the ability to work together toward a common vision. The ability to direct individual

---

9   Peter Tollman, Josh Serlin, Michelle Akers, Anson Dorrance, "The Power of Inspiration, Perspiration, and Cooperation—in Sports and in Business," The Boston Consulting Group, June 13, 2018, https://www.bcg.com/publications/2018/power-inspiration-perspiration-cooperation-sports-business.aspx.

accomplishment toward organizational objectives. It is the fuel that allows common people to attain uncommon results." When a team is committed to the organization's purpose, they will follow the directions that will get them to achieve it. Purpose clearly defines what a team's priorities are.

Take, for example, a fast food restaurant that made it their purpose to make impact hires. It was the restaurant's strong and stated purpose to give second chances to those who needed one. Imagine that a felon was recently released from jail and was wearing an ankle monitoring device while on parole, unable to find a job anywhere until the restaurant owner hired him. Understanding the value of the purpose that the restaurant had (and being grateful for it!), would you be surprised if he did the job so well that he quickly moved all the way up the ladder to general manager in two years? Purpose would drive the new hire and his fellow workers to be deeply engaged with their work. The restaurant would have award-winning customer service, as well as revenue.

Consistently, studies show that effective teams invest the time required for the team members to discuss and agree on a purpose that provides the team's directions. Jean Wyatt and Terry Hamm, school teachers with a purpose to impact students' lives, captured this concept when they simply said to their students (and future leaders), "People support that in which they have a hand in creating." Thus, a leader needs to collaborate with their team in order to create an authentic higher calling that inspires.

## Communicate Consistently

When a leader takes the time to get buy-in from the team members, everyone is on the same proverbial page. Then the leader should consistently remind the team about their purpose, mission, and vision. Staying on message keeps the team focused and informed when distractions arise. Without this clear and frequent communication, performance could be undermined.

Purpose should be embedded in company culture, the DNA of an organization. To actively and visually remind employees, one healthcare CEO starts every meeting with a slide stating the organization's purpose, mission, vision, and values. The purpose focuses the organization, prioritizes employees' attention, and identifies what is important. It helps when team members express the purpose with their own contributions. In doing so, employees engage with the purpose; it is not just words on the conference room wall; instead, they know why their place on this specific team is important. Knowing where the team is headed and why, team members put forth their best effort. They understand their true north.

A group of young professionals furthered their purpose when they decided to give back to their community by starting a grassroots nonprofit organization. The original purpose came from their cherished memories of camp in their youth and their desire to provide these same experiences to develop other kids' sense of worth during their developmental years. Because all the workers were moonlighting, all the funds they raised went directly to realizing this mission, meaning that the founders, board, and volunteers did all the work at night and on weekends for no compensation. They targeted two specific groups who would probably not have the camp experience without the organization's help: orphans and then the widows and children of fallen heroes. As the founders grew and had kids of their own, the nonprofit's strong purpose cascaded to new leaders who today continue the mission of inspiring youth through the camp adventure. The nonprofit's sustainability is directly attributed to the passion that the founders had for its purpose.

## Execute a Strategy

The next principle for building a powerhouse is to execute a strategy. USWNT Coach Tony DiCicco said, "There's more to the game of soccer, to any sport for that matter, than simply x's and o's. It's about competing. It's about winning. But perhaps most of all, it's about having fun and enjoying the journey along the way."[10] Coaches have to solve the strategic problem of how to position their players on the field. Researchers tend to characterize soccer teams' strategies as the extent of offense or defense (behavior) by each half of the game.[11] Basically, teams that attack more will score more goals but also have more goals scored against them. Based on the strategic decision that each team chose, the researchers estimated the team's probabilities of scoring, as well as conceding goals to the other team. Kristine's team member Christie Rampone simplified this strategy when she said, "If we score, we might win. If they never score, we can't lose."

It turns out, the studies show that the coaches' choice between an offense or defense strategy is not optimal, as they are far more conservative than the

---

10  Tony DiCicco, Colleen Hacker, *Catch Them Being Good* (New York: Penguin Books, 2002).

11  Ricardo Manuel Santos, "Optimal Soccer Strategies," *Economic Inquiry* 52, no. 1 (2014).

optimal strategy model predicts they should be. A more aggressive attacking offensive strategy would be better in more cases than a conservative defensive strategy where you position more players in front of your goal to prevent the other team from scoring. Even though the conservative defensive strategy is less than optimal for teams to adopt, teams continue to trend to more defensive strategies, resulting in a decline in the number of goals scored. To explain this deviation from optimal behavior, we need to look at why coaches choose their actual strategy. One possibility is that the coach is unable to correctly evaluate the decision between an offensive/defensive strategy and the probability of goals. Or, it could be that the coach is risk averse and prefers a safer strategy.

At halftime, Kristine's team members would share what they felt on the field, and then the coach provided new directions based on the players' perspectives. Researchers assessed coaches' halftime adjustments like this to show that when a team is winning at halftime, the second-half optimal strategy depends on other factors, like the game's location and quality of their opponent. When playing on an away field versus a stronger opponent, it is more optimal to have a defensive strategy. If you're on home field versus an equal or weaker opponent, it is better to have an offensive strategy. Kristine's team tended to have an attacking mentality and go after the other team, regardless if they were at home or on the road.

Most teams behave consistently with rationality and equilibrium. The one factor that tends to be more psychological is home field advantage, which brings a significant effect on the probability of scoring. Kristine won the World Cup in California and the Olympics in Atlanta, where her team had home field advantage both times. The best teams know how to respond to their situation and adjust their strategy in order to continue to win. Kristine and her team also won without home field advantage—in 1991 while in China for the World Cup and 2004 in Greece for the Olympics.

FIFA (The Fédération Internationale de Football Association), an international governing body, does not want defensive strategies to prevail. Instead, the organization would prefer that teams use more offensive strategies so that more goals are scored during games. They believe that by producing more goals, similar to basketball and American football, matches will be better and attract more consumer interest in soccer. To encourage this change in behavior, FIFA changed the rules in 1995 to encourage more offensive strategies. The three-point rule, which in a tournament gives 3 points instead of 2 points per victory (1 for tie and 0 for loss), is meant to drive more offensive strategy.[12]

## Be Agile in a Dynamic Market

There is a common phrase in the army that goes, "Your battle plan is only good until the first shot is fired." Your plan of attack can be similar in soccer, in that your game plan is only good until the other team scores. It is fairly obvious that your competitor's performance in soccer is based on the goals scored against you. You cannot ignore the opponent's score when making game decisions.

In the business world, companies must stay ahead of the game if they want to have a fighting chance. They decide how aggressive to be with a market penetration or expansion strategy. Do they decide to defend their current market position by warding off competitors, or do they attack new markets with new products and services? With big data and more sophisticated analytics becoming increasingly available, leaders make more informed decisions to optimize strategy by assessing what the probability of success is for each different scenario that they are considering. This probability of success is dependent both on the organization's capacity to execute their strategy, as well as their external business landscape and competitors.

The problem for many companies is that strategic planning is static, and they are essentially throwing in the towel to their competitors because they are not able to adapt quickly to market changes. Executive teams or boards meet annually to create a five-year plan. Instead, they need to meet more frequently, like soccer players at halftime, to assess their performance and make adjustments to their market direction. The team must be able to correctly measure the costs and benefits of a strategic decision and give their feedback to leadership. Just as players can help a coach adjust their defensive or offensive approach, so too can team members help risk-adverse executives make more informed decisions based on experiences in the field.

---

12 "Three Points for a Win," Wikipedia, accessed January 31, 2019, https://en.wikipedia.org/wiki/Three_points_for_a_win.

## Decide Where to Play, How to Win

One multinational consumer goods CEO was famous for his two-part strategy. First, he said you have to decide where to play. Essentially, you need to analyze and think critically about what industries are attractive for businesses to operate in. Not all industries are equal, and a good CEO will direct the business to attractive opportunities. Once you decide where to play, the second part of the strategy is to compete to win! The top companies competing in that industry receive the majority of the revenue and can scale effectively. This is where you want to be. You want to win the market share and customer preference.

Like FIFA's three-point rule change, industries are constantly shifting due to new regulations and changing incentives. Your organization must adjust to and leverage these disruptions. In the best case, doing so will keep you ahead of your competitors, and in the worst case it will keep you from falling behind.

Because you cannot expect that tomorrow's industry landscape will stay the same, executive teams must continually evaluate the environment to determine rising risks or incorrect assumptions about their strategies. This will help businesses make consistent strategic decisions. Keep these questions in mind: What is your home field advantage that will give you a competitive edge? What capabilities can you develop to compete more effectively? How did you execute against your strategic objectives?

# Solve Problems

The first problem a soccer team has to solve is how to get the ball from the other team. Kristine's team's overall direction had them utilize an attacking strategy, yet they also defended together with a defensive strategy to "double back." This meant that forwards would double back to help midfielders, and midfielders would double back to help defenders. All players had to double back to help out. Thus, an opposing player was always playing against two players from Kristine's team. When the USWNT followed this strategy, they would be more successful on winning the ball. Whenever they played other teams, they would shout "double" on the field. One time after playing Germany, a German player said during the post-game interview how much she and her teammates hated hearing the word "double"!

Just as a soccer coach decides on what strategy will be most effective with his or her players, a business leader must decide which strategy will work best for his or her team and organization's overall goals. In business, decision-making capabilities are the foundational skill needed to solve problems.

## Initiate Conversation

In every organization, how a team solves problems says a lot about the team, indicating if they are proactive or reactive, if they are data driven or emotion based, and if they are authoritarian or democratic. First and foremost, teams need to take initiative and recognize a problem without hiding from it. Indecision can harm your team as much as a poor decision. Many ant hills escalate into mountains of more serious issues, because they are not addressed when they are first observed. As popular men's soccer player Kyle Rote Jr. once said, "If you're attacking, you don't get as tired as when you're chasing."[13] Your team should attack problems head-on so you are not chasing the issue's impact later.

Having effective and direct problem-solving skills can prevent an issue spiraling into a catastrophe. Unresolved problems can keep teams from moving forward. Before an issue escalates, a team should analyze the situation and discuss solutions before it becomes more serious.

By realizing that many problems are part of a larger issue, teams can focus on specific, smaller issues to gain clarity as they work toward solving the more challenging/bigger issue at hand. When a team needs to make a decision, the clarified roles and trust built over time are critical. The decision should happen when and where the situation occurs. It is a process instead of people issue, so consider the "what" and not the "who." By bringing up the difficult conversations, they are addressing the unsaid and visualizing a positive outcome. As a leader, you can ask pointed questions to best address the issue, attacking it head-on, as Rote suggests.

---

13  Kory Avaiusini, "Attack Don't Chase: Soccer offers a lesson on how to aquire and retain the best talent," *Seattle Business Magazine*, accessed January 31, 2019, https://www.seattlebusinessmag.com/business-corners/workplace/attack-dont-chase-soccer-offers-lesson-how-acquire-and-retain-best-talent.

## Analyze Cause and Effect

When teams are analyzing situations, they should be thinking about the causes and effects of preceding events. Assess why there are progress roadblocks, and brainstorm how the team can overcome them, go through them, or remove them.

The consequences of decisions, both long and short term, should also be considered. The team should be rational and intuitive when making a decision, gathering as many facts and perspectives as time allows. As a leader, you should help them evaluate the potential solution option, consider risks versus benefits, and prepare for action. You'll all be the better for it.

### A Note about Group Think

One concern with a tight-knit and cohesive team is that they might not encourage each other to give constructive feedback or look for new ways to improve. They might run the risk of creating a "country club" atmosphere, where team players aspire toward harmony without rocking the boat and prioritize "go along to get along." This sort of team culture results in "group think," where a team becomes closed minded.

While this harmonious environment is pleasant, it may not be good for work or the overall objectives of the team or organization. Yes, your team could appear happy, engaged, and content on the surface; however, if you look deeper, you will see that an artificial cohesiveness has been created.

Chances are, in order for a team to improve, you'll need to disrupt the status quo. If you instead succumb to group think, your team will limit facts, ignore risks, dismiss valuable external perspectives, and not consider potential solutions.

Teams can minimize group think by initiating conversation, leveraging experience, assigning a respectful dissenter, and analyzing team actions. Ultimately, you need a team that makes good decisions that are effective, not a bunch of "yes men" who agree to whatever they are told. Instead they raise good questions, bring light to better solutions, and build consensus.

## Leverage Team Experience

Teams should leverage their experience and expertise to gather information that is relevant and specific. The expression "two heads are better than one" comes into play, as team members working in tandem can contribute to a better possible solution than what only one person could have conceived. Many teams underutilize the individual talents. This untapped knowledge, skill, and ability is "sitting on the bench" and not contributing to the performance of the team. Usually the leader is unaware of those assets, or she does not know how to allocate the work responsibilities in order to harness these individual capabilities so team performance is optimized.

As a leader, challenge group think and make the tough decisions for the greater good of the team. This, in turn, will challenge the group's thinking, beliefs, and assumptions. Pay specific attention to actively pulling the introvert's perspective to the group, as that person could hesitate to share. Of course, to have willing contributions, each team member's suggestion should be respected and considered, even if not chosen. Do not discourage the alternative perspectives; instead, encourage the disagreement when the discussion leads to a better solution. By pulling various perspectives, innovative ideas, and unique opinions together, the solution is more validated due to the team's efforts. Play devil's advocate and be skeptical. And if you need to, find an outside source to provide a different perspective.

## Size Your Team

As you acquire more team members, keep in mind that team size affects team functioning and can lead to additional problems. A larger team has growing challenges, such as complicating communication, decreasing quality of interactions, and increasing coordination requirements. As the team size grows, the focus on communication, interaction, and coordination becomes pivotal. All too often, larger teams complain of "not being in the know," because communications do not occur frequently enough or to the level desired by those team members. Bigger is not necessarily better, as the team issues encountered advance exponentially with size increases. So, team size should be limited to the number of members required for maximum impact. Before adding a person to the team, the leader should validate that a proposed team member has a knowledge, skill, or ability to contribute that the team does not currently have.

There is a balance between including the right team members who have expertise to contribute and a stake in the result, and not letting the group making the decision become unwieldy because it is too big. Laszlo Bock, when he was senior vice president of people operations at Google, said, "It's feeling the sense of responsibility, the sense of ownership, to step in, to try to solve any problem—and the humility to step back and embrace the better ideas of others. Your end goal is what can we do together to problem solve. I've contributed my piece, and then I step back."[14] Too many cooks in the kitchen is not effective for problem solving. Also, there should be clarity on decisions that are not subject to team consensus, and instead the authority is delegated to one specific team member's role to be accountable for.

## Prioritize Your "First Team"

For many executive teams, you see this risk play out in their siloed thinking of individual department responsibility instead of taking a holistic perspective and collaborating for the collective benefit. When an executive's loyalty to their department is greater than the executive team, it intensifies the "silo" business function divisions within the company and magnifies the problems not solved. They build their empire, protect their turf, do not communicate, and jockey for promotion. They prefer to stand out and be distinguished rather than work together. Basically, they escalate functional versus enterprise tension. This is quite evident during budgeting allocation when each department attempts to maximize their budget while blinded to the overall business needs. Strong egos compete for their own interests, even if taking a larger share of the pie hinders other team members' contributions to the company.

Instead, when leaders view the executive team as their "first team," they put the company's interests above themselves and their department. They encourage a holistic organizational perspective that is broader than their business unit. An executive must be willing to subordinate their own goals and interests,

---

14  Jeanine Prime and Elizabeth Salib, "The Best Leaders Are Humble Leaders," *Harvard Business Review*, May 12, 2014, https://hbr.org/2014/05/the-best-leaders-are-humble-leaders.

moving from independent to interdependent. The same is true for employees, who should put the well-being of the team above their own interests.

In order for a powerhouse to effectively align toward a team direction, you will need these three principles of purpose, strategy, and problem solving that Marissa Mayer has executed well at Google, Yahoo!, and now Lumi Labs.

# 1:1 with Marissa Mayer

Marissa Mayer is cofounder of Lumi Labs, an organization that builds consumer applications enabled by artificial intelligence. She was previously president and chief executive officer of Yahoo!, as well as a Google executive. At thirty-three years old, she was the youngest woman listed as one of America's Most Powerful Women in Business by Fortune. She is on many corporate and nonprofit boards, as well as an active technology company investor.

## How does a company establish purpose and reason for their teams to follow?

Company purpose all comes down to vision. The leader develops and conveys the vision and the mission—what are you trying to achieve. The vision and mission lay out what the future looks like. The team enrolls themselves in that vision as they work, accomplish, make, and create value for the group and organization.

Ultimately, this process is a collaboration. At Google, we were a start-up creating our purpose. Coming into an established organization at Yahoo! that already had an existing purpose was different. Our leadership team would hold a weekly meeting with the entire company to share information and provide a forum for input and questions.

## How does a company effectively establish and execute strategy?

The vision and purpose lead to the strategy and tactics. Make this feel as collaborative as possible by establishing open communication top-down and bottoms-up.

The general process that I feel works well is to share what would be the most important achievements for the next year as well as the biggest challenges. Then, we would have town hall meetings, input meetings, and calls for ideas. Team members would develop their ideas for new projects, and then submit ideas for consideration. The leadership would receive presentations to learn more about each idea that was submitted (i.e., Google Maps and Gmail at Google, or the ad unit at Yahoo!).

Then, the leadership team hashes through the ideas, determining what are the best and most impactful ideas, as well as what we could afford to fund. The feedback cycle was a closed loop, with immediate sharing of why someone's idea was not selected so that they could improve this submission or the next one.

Once decisions were finalized around which projects were part of the next year's strategy, we would then build a tactical financial plan. The leadership would take the strategy and plan back to the company, explaining which initiatives we were pursuing, why they were the most strategically important, and the best positioned to succeed.

Employees were invested in the process. They wanted to participate, learn, and understand what was chosen. Everyone wants to make progress and make an impact.

At Lumi Labs, it is the same process, just a different scale. We are faster and smaller. What might happen at a larger company on a quarterly basis in terms of tradeoffs and decisions can occur at a start-up daily.

## When your company has a problem to solve, how do you effectively make the decision?

I try to make sure the right person on the team is making the decision. You want the people who work most directly on the problem to be the most involved. If a decision can be delegated, then it should absolutely be delegated. When you give decisions to the team to make, this increases team participation, responsibility, and accountability, and it's very strengthening to the team.

Then, you need to make sure that you have the best available information to help make the decision.

The two biggest things for good decision making are having the relevant information and that the right person is making the decision.

# Tactics for Your Team

To align a powerhouse's direction, you need to make sure your team members have a sense of raison d'être so that everyone gives extra effort because they understand the significance of their work. You must also execute a sound strategy so you can continuously evaluate and implement your plan. And last, you must be ready to solve problems so you can address issues as they surface.

> With these three principles in mind, take a moment to consider how you will:
>
> **1.** Understand and identify the fundamental reason and purpose that the company is in business for?
>
> **2.** Execute a plan to succeed?
>
> **3.** Make high-quality decisions to address issues?

*There is nothing like celebrating a goal with your teammates. Here Carli Lloyd, Stephanie Lopez, and Kristine share a group hug after a goal. They went on to beat Mexico 5–0 at Gillette Stadium in Foxborough on April 14, 2007. (Credit: Howard C. Smith/isiphotos.com)*

# Scoring a Goal

*"My short-term specific goals remained my focus,
as I knew that if I took care of these goals,
then my stretch goals would be achieved in time."*

**—Carli Lloyd**

P art of being a high achiever is having a clearly defined idea of what
you want to achieve. Not only is it important to have a goal to strive
toward, it's crucial that once you have it in your head that you commit
to attaining it. USWNT Coach Tony DiCicco once said, "When you set a goal,
write it down, and then it's like making a promise to yourself."[15]

When Kristine reflects on how she set her life goals as a promising soccer
player in her teens, she notes that at the time she did not have an ultimate
goal of playing on the USWNT—it did not exist. However, she did have the
dream that many young athletes have, to be in the Olympics. When she was
younger, there was no women's soccer in the Olympics, but as a young girl
she saw Nadia Comaneci compete in gymnastics and thought maybe one day
she too could compete in the Olympics. With the dream to win gold in the

---

15   Tony DiCicco, Colleen Hacker, *Catch Them Being Good* (New York: Penguin Books, 2002).

back of her head, she set out to accomplish smaller, more specific goals first. In order to contribute to her team's success, her objectives were about individual preparation, working hard, and making a difference. Later, when she was on the USWNT, she and her teammates had a constant mission: to win. Not just the World Cup or the Olympics, but every game, even "friendlies." For them, every game was a reflection on their team's capability, as well as an opportunity for them to work together. They felt there was no reason to not play 100 percent all of the time. They did not slack off their goal to win, and the results speak for themselves. Kristine remembers the collective team mindset about all their games. "Every game mattered. It always mattered. If we let anyone have an inch, it would change their view of us. We wanted the other countries to be scared of the US—to think we were invincible. Therefore, we played with intensity every game. We took nothing for granted. We had confidence in the team. We did not want any team to believe that they could beat us."

## Why Goal Setting Is Important

Goals are important for all of us in any stage of life. They motivate performance and often inspire team members to give additional effort. When a team works together to achieve a common goal, everyone benefits.

As the Cheshire Cat in *Alice's Adventures in Wonderland* said, "If you don't know where you're going, then any road will get you there." Specific goals help strengthen the team's direction and focus, because the team can visualize what success looks like. Vague goals do not challenge team members, nor do they clarify responsibility, and they make the future state as clear as mud.

## Set Specific Goals

A research study on soccer players was done to assess the impact of setting specific objectives to improve ball-handling skills. The participants' ball handling improved noticeably after setting goals to define three specific behaviors: movement with the ball, movement during restarts, and movement after passes. Even when the time period of the study was over, the players' movement with the ball was maintained near the desired level, demonstrating that the practice helped them improve the new skill long term.[16] This goal-setting process was successful because players had objective performance measurements. In sports settings, a specific performance goal, set either by the athlete or coach, is critical.

## Be Clear

Setting specific goals for your team helps them understand what it is they need to master or undertake in order to achieve. For example, we often hear the phrase, "do your best"—a generic and ambiguous encouragement. For someone who hears this advice, although they might know that a leader has high expectations for their performance, they have no clear picture of what "your best" would look like. Research shows that specific and clear goals always outperform the more general goals.[17] If a manager were to say something like, "Do your best to improve your contract closes for the next month," they would provide explicit criteria to strive toward. The individual then has a clear sense of direction when working toward achieving their specific goal. As you help your team develop, identify a limited number of specific goals that will most differentiate the team performance, and strive to help your team overcome any barriers on their journey to achieving them. Attainable goals are more realistic, with a high probability of being successful in the short term.

## Define Priorities

A specific and focused approach will help teams agree on the steps they need to take, helping them more consistently achieve and accomplish their purpose. If competing priorities threaten to interrupt team progress, the team can review their goals to get back on track. Clearly defined goals make it easier for teams to know which actions are necessary.

---

16  Brandilea Brobst and Phillip Ward, "Effects of Public Posting, Goal Setting, and Oral Feedback on the Skills of Female Soccer Players," *Journal of Applied Behavior Analysis* 35, no. 3 (Feb. 2002): 247–57.

17  Ethem Duygulu and Nurcan Ciraklar, "Effects of Leadership Roles on Team Effectiveness," *Journal of Economics, Administrative, International Relations and Political Science* 9, no. 2 (April 2009), https://www.researchgate.net/publication/227349625_Effects_of_Leadership_Roles_on_Team_Effectiveness.

In order to win, you must prioritize your goals to know where to act. One healthcare CEO's advice to help his team understand which actions should be prioritized is the motto "WIN," which stands for "**W**hat is **I**mportant **N**ow?" This advice helps his team focus on what they need to do in the present, rather than focusing too much on the future. By prioritizing the immediate need, this tactic helps teams overcome fear, procrastination, or conflict. A goal without a prioritized plan is just a wish.

## Individual vs. Team Goals

Individual goals contribute to team goals, as they dictate individual action. Whether your goal is an advanced degree, a new job, or a promotion, you will have something concrete to focus on. Individual metrics for business goals could include a sales quota, a call center response rate, or the number of billable hours to a client. These individual responsibilities address identified team needs, as well as align the individual to the same page as everyone else on the team.

Yet, there is a disconnect between the focus on teams to achieve the organization's goals and the awarding of individual performance. For many companies, an individual's incentives are not aligned with the team's collective goals. Typically, goal setting is part of the annual performance management review process that companies conduct for their employees. For most organizations, these reviews are focused only on individual performance. This is because the employees are compensated with salary and bonuses for individual accomplishments instead of team rewards that require collaboration.

A performance management process that rewards individually is similar to a college class having a team project and then giving a different grade to each student. The individual incentive is not aligned to the team's and rewards task responsibility and completion over teamwork skills like collaborating, building trust, and developing others. While the individual could do his or her job well to accomplish individual goals and be affirmed for it in the performance management system, the failure to contribute to team goals is not considered.

Employees are rarely incentivized to be good team members, as most companies do not award collective recognition for achieving the team goal. This common approach is detrimental to a tight-knit team, as it does not encourage a team member to desire and aspire for better team performance. Instead, you should include an employee's teaming ability in your performance management process. Through reinforcement, incentives, and rewards, a team member develops better teamwork capabilities. Organizational performance is team driven, so why not reward the collective instead of the individual?

## Track Goal Achievement

Goals need metrics to help quantify how successful a team has been at achieving their desired results, or to help show them how far they may still need to go. These goals will also help differentiate your role and responsibility, making performance expectations clear. A team's commitment to their goals enables them to hit their stride, sustain, and then realize their purpose.

In addition, most performance management is long term, where research shows that a short-term goal with a current baseline will better resonate with an employee.[18] When an organization can implement a series of short-term individual goals, their employees will develop faster. Technologies that encourage real-time performance documentation integrated into the team's workflow are disrupting the historic annual performance management process, making goal setting and feedback more dynamic, inclusive, and robust. Companies now need a proactive leader to change the process to complement the technology.

## Stretch Goals

Often, most goals are not ambitious enough and do not push team members to leave it all on the field. There is not enough challenge to deliver high performance. The USWNT's ultimate goals of winning the World Cup and an Olympic gold medal fell under a "stretch category" of goal setting. A stretch goal is a goal that inspires an increased level of effort and innovative approaches. Kristine wanted her team to be the best, and this was always her goal. After each World Cup, they trained the next three years to win it the next time, making themselves stronger and faster. As Kristine's teammate Mia Hamm encourages, "Raise the bar a little higher each time you succeed."

---

18  Brandilea Brobst and Phillip Ward, "Effects of Public Posting, Goal Setting, and Oral Feedback on the Skills of Female Soccer Players," *Journal of Applied Behavior Analysis* 35, no. 3 (February 2002): 247–57.

Kristine's teammate Abby Wambach captured the essence of stretch goals when she said, "It's a beautiful thing to watch people push themselves further than they think they can." The USWNT was able to achieve its stretch goal of multiple World Cup wins by setting smaller, realistic, and more attainable goals that were more immediate and would help them get to their larger stretch goal. By working toward attaining these incremental goals, their achievement determined if they would win/lose on their ultimate goal.

First, they had individual preparation goals, such as being fit, healthy, and energized. Second were performance goals. As an attacking midfielder, Kristine needed to get to the opponent's "end line" at least five times during a game to increase her team's probability of scoring a goal. To ensure she was improving on this front, she had a team member on the bench track her "end line" number during a game. When reviewing her success or failure of achieving that metric after each game, she then assessed where she missed an opportunity to reach her goal and made a mental note to course-correct for the next time.

Third, for efficiency purposes, the USWNT coaches also created microteams, or "small societies" of player groupings. They gave each group a label, such as "forwards," "midfielders," or "defenders." These microteams had a specific role to help the team win, whether that was scoring a goal or keeping the other team from scoring a goal. The coaches would set specific objectives for each microteam that could only be achieved if each team member worked together. The goal setting was structured so that if each microteam succeeded during the game, then they should win that particular game. Of course, theory and practice are two entirely different things, and they didn't always achieve all of their microteam goals in any given game or win every match.

The USWNT had a solid plan in place, assessed their delivery after each game, and took strides to improve on their attainable goals as individuals, microteams, and a team. Because of this, they were able to achieve their ultimate stretch goal of winning the World Cup Championship multiple times (1991, 1999, 2015) and, also impressively, they won the Olympic gold medal four of the first five times (1996, 2004, 2008, 2012).

## Challenge Your Team

Stretch goals should be those goals that challenge your business teams to achieve something tomorrow that you can't quite reach today. A-Team players want to do something extraordinary, to demonstrate their exceptional capability and competent dedication. Typically, a stretch goal tends to motivate the individual more, whereas modest goals do not. When your team has a star to reach for, they will work hard to achieve.

## Balance Goals

Similar to sports, businesses need both immediate specific and long-term stretch goals to develop your team to its fullest potential. Keep these goals balanced. When setting a goal, a leader should look both at what the team needs as well as what the individual's strengths and aspirations are. Once the goal is set, the employee should agree and accept the goal so they're aligned with the leader and have buy-in with the goal. Team members need to care about achieving the goal.

These agreed-upon goals by the team member and leader are the basic blueprints that illustrate what actions are required from the team member. These explicit goals should align to the department's and company's purpose and goals.

## Track Goals

Team leaders should conduct periodic status checks to review goal progress to help keep employees on track to achieving their goals. A believable measurement system with fair metrics can help determine whether their goals are getting closer to fruition or not. When team members accomplish their goals, the sense of accomplishment contributes significantly to employee motivation, job satisfaction, and engagement. They feel more competent and capable, as well as ready for the next goal.

If the goal is not finite, a leader should work with their employee to determine what milestones can be measured to track progress and guide the team member on what actions they can take. Putting short-term "quick wins" at the beginning of the project can help the team build momentum. Teams have self-fueling spirals, so you want them to be going up instead of down. Early successes will cause teams to aspire for more as well as increase their faith in their capabilities.

When team members do not accomplish their goals, disappointment sets in. After all, there are consequences if the goal is not met. They may feel they are being judged on the results, which are unfavorable. This can be a learning opportunity; of course, the team member has to take responsibility first before they can learn from their failure. Thus, leaders need to make sure and choose an appropriate goal difficulty so that employees do not become frustrated.

## Create a Competitive Environment

Teams flourish in a competitive environment, where positive peer pressure drives each team member to improve their individual performance. In this kind of space, individual improvement benefits overall team achievement by encouraging all team members to increase their standards and contribution to the team. However, the culture of the team must be characterized by trust so that team members see beyond the individual competition to the larger team impact of winning more.

To create a competitive environment, start posting goals publicly. Sharing an individual or team goal with everyone drives accountability. Coach Dorrance once said, "What's critical for me as a coach is to recruit every single element to drive performance."[19] He meticulously tracked his players' performance, and his team members were always competitive with each other. For example, he posted the speed ladder on the board in their locker room, indicating who was the fastest and who was the slowest on the team. No one ever wanted to be last on the list, so everyone tried to run faster.

Every week at practice, to build their mental strength, Coach Dorrance had his players compete in one-on-one competitions that were exhausting. Then, after the drill, the players had to stand in the front of the group and describe their performance outcome. If the individual had won all of the competitions, she could proudly say "3–0." If, however, she had lost her competitions, then she had to say "0–3." This built responsibility and accountability for everyone's individual efforts.

With these methods, Coach Dorrance instilled a healthy level of competition among his team. They always wanted to be better. It was about competing,

---

19  Peter Tollman, Josh Serlin, Michelle Akers, Anson Dorrance, "The Power of Inspiration, Perspiration, and Cooperation—in Sports and in Business," The Boston Consulting Group, June 13, 2018, https://www.bcg.com/publications/2018/power-inspiration-perspiration-cooperation-sports-business.aspx.

not just against others, but also themselves, so that every day on the field, they could bring their best. It was good to be around these A Players, as they all wanted to be the best, wanted to win, and hated to lose. Coach Dorrance refers to this phenomenon as a "competitive environment." He did a great job of balancing this on-the-field competition with off-the-field camaraderie; otherwise, they would have been a collection of individuals competing for self-statistics instead of a team playing to win.

Research shows that the public posting of goals is an effective behavioral strategy to improve performance. The public posting, in addition to constructive feedback provided to the performer, both prompts and reinforces performance. These studies show performance improvements in sports from public posting that range from reducing absenteeism, eliminating late arrivals and early departures, increasing the work rate, increasing the practice and game performance, and reducing illegal and improper behaviors.[20]

## Increase Transparency

In business, when you have specific goals that are posted, your team knows what to prepare for, what to practice, and what to perform. For many companies, the only public posting happens in call centers or sales departments. For all other jobs, most do not post, because they struggle to measure individual or team effectiveness. Every team should have a plan to post their goals as well as the high-level performance data on progress to achieving their goals.

On a broader scale, you could also incorporate a sense of corporate accountability by publicly posting employee engagement survey results. Employees would appreciate the transparency, as well as the open attempts at improving the workplace experience. As an example, a financial services corporation's engagement results were given to managers to show their team's strengths and areas for development. It was then the manager's responsibility to address those identified areas for improvement during the year, and the following year's engagement results indicated if those efforts were productive. In addition, each team saw their team results compared to the overall

---

20  Brandilea Brobst and Phillip Ward, "Effects of Public Posting, Goal Setting, and Oral Feedback on the Skills of Female Soccer Players," *Journal of Applied Behavior Analysis* 35, no. 3 (February 2002): 247–57.

company scores. Through this engagement survey process that included public posting, the company transparently improved its work environment.

## Post Outcomes Publicly

Not only the public posting of goals but also what a team member is going to do to improve their performance is what matters most. Wouldn't it be great if each individual's results were posted so that everyone would know who the 2 percent are that drive the company's business performance? These team members would earn respect from their colleagues. This practice would also show who the team loafers were and could further inspire others to do better in the workplace. One global technology company does this by posting all employees' current and past goals on their internal employee directory. This directory lists their name, title, contact information, and then their goals.

Encouraging competition in the workplace has pros and cons. Some call this the gamification of work. Many companies see benefits when they structure friendly teams and competitions instead of pitting individuals against each other. This team-based approach helps build camaraderie, as the teammates have a common goal. Similar to soccer practice, the ideal is pushing everyone's performance to an even higher level. Every team has some degree of competition, so there is a need to channel that toward external competitors to avoid compromising the team's internal collaboration. This competitive workplace sharpens each other's capabilities to then focus on winning in the marketplace.

USWNT co-captain Carli Lloyd is a prolific goal scorer. In the interview that follows, you will learn more about how Carli scores goals for her team by using these three goal-setting principles: specific goals, stretch goals, and a competitive environment.

## 1:1 with Carli Lloyd

In the 2015 World Cup, Carli Lloyd helped her team become world champions when she scored a hat trick against Japan—three goals in one game. In this performance, one of her goals was an extremely long shot from midfield. She is a two-time Olympic gold medalist, as well as the FIFA Player of the Year in 2015 and 2016.

## How did having specific goals help your career?

Growing up I never really had any direction as to how to train and never had any specific goals to reach for. My broad goal was to play on the Women's National Team, but I had no real plan as to how I would get there. It was after I started working with my personal coach, James Galanis of Universal Soccer Academy, that I laid down a plan with specific goals. James evaluated my game and made me aware of my strengths and weaknesses and then designed a plan to improve my strengths and to turn my weaknesses into strengths. Some of my specific goals were to become a lot more efficient when in possession of the ball, to become better at tactically understanding the game, to build a solid base of endurance, to study the mental toughness skills of a champion, and to build character skills that would help me deal with adversity in a positive way. Conquering these specific goals not only helped me conquer my bigger goals but also made me realize that you need specific and stretch goals in order to be the best version of you.

## When did you make stretch goals?

Having achieved my specific goals allowed me to make my debut for the US Women's National Team and helped me eventually gain a starting spot in the lineup. As my confidence grew, I realized that I was going to play a big part on the field, and with this I started to establish my stretch goals. These goals included becoming top goal scorer, leading the team with assists, winning the Olympics, winning the World Cup, and ultimately winning the World Player of the Year award. My short-term specific goals remained my focus, as I knew that if I took care of these goals, then my stretch goals would be achieved in time.

## What is it like being in a competitive environment?

I love being in a competitive environment. It helps not only me but also the entire team in terms of improving. When you know that you cannot have an off day at training because there will be someone there to take your spot—it pushes you to break barriers.

When you're invited into a national team camp, you are there with up to forty players looking to make it into the squad of twenty. This creates healthy competition and tests your mental strength. If you've performed well, you make the twenty-person squad and then begin the process of competing for a spot in the starting eleven. If you make the eleven, then you have to play at your peak or your spot will be taken instantly. The competition that exists and has existed with the USWNT has played a big role in the success of our women's program here in the USA. You have to love competing in order to be successful. In my time with the US Women's National Team, I cannot remember a time feeling comfortable that I have cemented my spot, and this has helped grow my game continuously over time.

## Tactics for Your Team

Building a powerhouse comes from being focused on scoring goals. These goals should be specific to align team activity. A team should also have stretch goals balanced with attainable goals so they can achieve small victories in the short term, while simultaneously challenging themselves to achieve greatness and more challenging victories in the long term. And last, goals should be publicized and shared with the team to hold all members accountable in a competitive environment.

Consider how you can implement these practices in your own organization. How will you:

1. Specify the desired outcome and prioritize it?

2. Challenge your team with a high standard for success?

3. Review and track each team member's goals and performance accomplishments?

Pillar 2:

# EMPOWER

After your team transforms, leadership needs to empower the team. Setting the team foundation enables the team to act with authority. Leading a team means entrusting different individuals to leverage their strengths to guide and influence others. If you're leading on an international team, you'll also delegate across boundaries and borders by granting cross-cultural variances. A powerhouse needs strong leadership to perform at its highest level.

*This photo of Anson Dorrance was taken at Kristine's Hall of Fame induction on February 14, 2015. She asked Anson, the man who changed her life when she was sixteen years old, to introduce her and, without hesitation, he obliged. (Credit: Doug Zimmerman/isiphotos.com)*

# Setting the Team Foundation

*"A champion is someone who is bent over,*
*drenched in sweat, at the point of exhaustion,*
*when no one else is watching."*

—**Anson Dorrance**

C oach Anson Dorrance is the father of women's soccer in the United States. Kristine remembers the feeling of being on his teams, saying, "Once you stepped on that field, you knew you were playing for more than just your country, you were playing for each other. Coach Dorrance always told us we were the best, and we believed it and showed it when we stepped out on the field." His coaching style was motivational, supportive, and challenging. He coached the USWNT from 1986 to 1994, setting the team's foundation from the moment he started working.

In any sport, you hear of coaching trees—where the coaches learn their vocation. Coach Dorrance built a coaching tree through his players. Developing them as great players and subsequently great coaches, Coach Dorrance's players have succeeded in the collegiate and USWNT coaching ranks, some being Angela Kelly, head coach at The University of Texas; Carla Overbeck, assistant coach at Duke University; Tiffany Roberts, head coach at the University of Central

Florida; Carin Gabarra, head coach at the United States Naval Academy; and April Heinrichs, head coach of the USWNT, to name a few.

Let's consider the extreme pressure on coaches. They experience a wide range of emotions: personal highs when the team wins, self-doubt and feelings of underachieving when the team loses. These pressures are especially evident at collegiate and national levels, where field performance—how many games you win—is the prime interest of sport teams.

Coaches are held responsible for their teams' successes and failures, wins and losses. This is especially so in professional sports, where your win/loss record affects each team's financial revenues. Winning teams usually have more revenue than weaker teams. If your team is not winning, then you'll have a lower ranking, which indirectly affects revenue by reduced ticket sales, merchandising, and sponsorships.

If the coach does not produce winning teams, the team replaces the coach. As the amount of revenue has increased in sports, including soccer, the pressure and turnover of coaches has increased, too. Teams hoping to improve field performance and team ranking are quicker to replace a coach. So, while a coach has tremendous pressure to win games or possibly lose their job, he/she also has to win on the field by motivating every member on the team.[21]

Coach Dorrance set his teams' foundation by always striving to inspire, setting expectations, and developing their talent. As a result he was able to lead his players to twenty-one NCAA national collegiate championships at The University of North Carolina, where he was named coach of the year seven times. As the USWNT coach for eight years, he won over 70 percent of his games, including the first-ever Women's World Cup in 1991 in China.

## Why the Team Foundation Is Important

In the business world, a coach or manager aligns team efforts so that they can accomplish company goals. The manager provides an internal and external point of view to the team that helps assess processes, address existing or potential issues, and assist with team dynamics. These managers are forward looking, with a results-oriented perspective that focuses on goals. They help the team

---

21  Anne-Line Balduck, Anita Prinzie, Marc Buelens, "The effectiveness of coach turnover and the effect on home team advantage, team quality and team ranking," *Journal of Applied Statistics* 37, no. 4 (2010).

debrief and understand the team's successes and failures. Like the coaches on the field, these business coaches are there to lead their teams to a "win" by collaborating and maximizing synergies.

When a leader effectively sets a foundation, they must build on solid ground: rock instead of sand. To build a solid, rock-firm base for their team, a leader should effectively inspire the team, set clear expectations, and develop talent. Without these actions, the foundation is more like sand and the team's performance will be unstable.

An example of a situation where the leader did not set the team foundation was when a global hotel chain sold their physical assets to a private equity (PE) firm and kept the employees on a management service contract. Yet, the new leader was not invested in operations, and the employees saw his disengagement. Everyone followed their own personal goals, as the team interests were not aligned and no one was on the same page. Employees showed up as zombies and took two-hour lunches. They sabotaged each other's work. Not surprisingly, the PE firm did not reach their projected profit margins. The result was a train wreck, predictably caused by a leader who did not inspire others, set expectations, or develop the team.

Contrast that with a CEO who did set the team foundation by focusing on product quality. One day, he was walking through the assembly plant and saw that one of the finished products had a slight imperfection. To make a point about the expectations he had about product quality, he went over to the end of the assembly line and destroyed that product. This action was extreme, yet the story went viral throughout the company. By doing this, he set a team foundation: quality was essential, and any imperfection was not acceptable. He inspired his team to strive for quality. This shows how a decisive action can set expectations for the team. This leader's behavior was much more impactful than a "value" being posted on the wall. Leaders of highly effective teams set the team foundation to be steady as a rock through inspiring, setting expectations, and developing talent.

## Inspire Others

Coaches should inspire others, encouraging hard work in the spirit of ultimate team dedication. When the leader inspires, followers will work hard because they understand the purpose that they are collaborating to achieve.

One of Coach Dorrance's coaching secrets to inspire his players was a hand-written letter. On the night before championship games at UNC, he took pen to paper and wrote a letter to each of the senior players on his team. In each, he detailed the ways in which the player had contributed to the team, how they had grown into women, and what his aspirations for them were after college. This example goes to show how he gave each of these players his heart: the experiences, memories, and friendships that they built from when he recruited them in high school through their four years at Chapel Hill. As you can imagine, these players gave everything the next day at the championship game. They would have run through walls if he'd asked them to!

## Encourage through Recognition

In business, the same thing can happen. Employees and teammates can also be motivated to perform. Most people can tell you which of their colleagues "perform" only when being watched by managers. However, we need teammates that we can rely on to hit their deliverables, make milestones, and go the extra mile for team performance.

Some of the responsibility for performance is on the team member, and some of this falls to the leader who inspires them. As a leader, do you connect with your team members to tell them how they are valuable to the team? Like Coach Dorrance, do you share with them before "the game" on why they are important for the team's success?

A global company that does this well has a corporate tradition of leaders sharing "awards" with teammates who have contributed. These awards are simple toys that have deeper meaning (i.e., when a teammate is "always on call to serve others" he might be given a toddler's toy phone). When you walk through their offices, people have a toy displayed with pride on their desks, as there is a specific value it shows they demonstrated. Each toy represents a leader inspiring a teammate through an award. Simple, yes. Effective, definitely!

## Use an Individualized Approach

A strong leader builds team member confidence and commitment one person at a time. Instead of checkers where each playing piece is the same, a leader who inspires is playing chess. Each team member has unique strengths and weaknesses, aspirations and experiences, and responsibilities that their manager can help shape. In addition, their leader can fill team capability gaps and explain how each member's contributions help the team accomplish their broader goal. Through this 1:1 approach, the leader personalizes the way he/she asks each team member to use their skills. All of this attention engages and inspires team members; they can become one with the team mission, which is contagious to other team members. Instead of a team member thinking "business as usual," they shift their mindset to "I feel important at work when . . ."

For many teams, team members are underutilized, as their talents are not fully understood by their leader and therefore untapped. Teams become strong when each member of the team is inspired to contribute their skill set for the benefit of the team. If an individual believes the leader is genuinely looking out for them, then they will more fully commit to the team and their performance improves. So, a leader's ability to motivate team members in the workplace is critical for effective teamwork. Casey Stengel, Major League Baseball manager, captured the challenge of inspiring team members when he said, "Gettin' good players is easy. Gettin' 'em to play together is the hard part."

## Set Clear Expectations

At the beginning of his tenure, Coach Dorrance made a powerful statement about the expectations of the UNC women's soccer culture. During the team's first practice, a player failed a fitness drill. He sent her home that evening, illustrating his clear expectation. After that, players understood that fitness was a prerequisite; the expectation was that they would be day-one ready.[22]

Setting expectations is key to the success of any team. Expectations aren't just words or rules; instead, they are standards that everyone must meet, every time. For Coach Dorrance, one of his core standards is that "principles drive behavior, not rules that tell us what to do."

---

22  Peter Tollman, Josh Serlin, Michelle Akers, Anson Dorrance, "The Power of Inspiration, Perspiration, and Cooperation—in Sports and in Business," The Boston Consulting Group, June 13, 2018, https://www.bcg.com/publications/2018/power-inspiration-perspiration-cooperation-sports-business.aspx.

## Create Operating Principles

The decisions and actions of leaders determine a company's culture. The leader sets expectations and establishes norms, laying the ground rules for success by clearly stating what an organization's operating principles are. These principles clarify what behaviors are expected and which ones are not allowed. The process creates a common language for a team to operate under. Each team member can also bring their personality and work experience to help shape and influence norms.

As an example, a police chief instructed the city's police officers that it was their responsibility to know and adhere to the policies that had been documented for all officers. It was not left open to interpretation; the policy was a commitment to behavior consistency across the entire police force. This makes sense when you consider that a police chief works eight hours a day, while the police force works in three shifts to cover a twenty-four-hour period. Most likely, criminal activity will occur when the chief is not working. In these situations when the police officer has to make a crucial decision, the officer should follow the set policies to keep everyone as safe as possible.

## Follow Through

Accountability is an important job function for coaches and leaders. Too often the desire to be liked outweighs the need to hold others accountable. What you allow, you enable. After setting expectations and establishing operating principles, a leader must follow through and call others out when they do not follow these expectations, or reward each team member that does. Clear rewards or sanctions are part of setting the foundation that team members need in order to have boundaries for their behavior. A leader must enforce their values and rules.

These expectations define how a team will accomplish its tasks. When expectations are unknown or compliance is ambiguous, teams will become ineffective. Vince Lombardi, the famous Green Bay Packers coach whom the NFL Super Bowl trophy is named after, said, "Individual commitment to a group effort—that is what makes a team work, a company work, a society work, a civilization work." Coach Lombardi understood that setting expectations for team members to commit to is critical for the team to be successful.

Too often, leaders say they value something, yet their decisions and actions say otherwise. If a leader does not follow through and enforce these expectations for themselves as well as their employees, they will not get the desired outcome and will have to course correct later. Consider an executive who values "career development" and then cuts the training budget, or a company that has "integrity" as a value but sells faulty products to clients. Why should the employees expect that the values mean anything? And why should employees listen to a company's values if their decisions and actions make it clear that the company doesn't really follow them?

## Walk the Talk

Contrast this with one CEO who gives out an award that's chattering teeth with two feet—it literally walked across employees' desks as a humorous visual acknowledgment to employees who demonstrated "walking the talk." He would get his point across to the entire company that culture is not just what you say. This particular award would be a clear and simple indication that he expected leaders to not only say what they valued but also to display their values with their behavior.

Like Coach Dorrance sending home an athletically unfit player from practice, a leader sets the expectations for the team. These leaders' behaviors were much more impactful than a "value" being posted on the wall; it was an example of them walking the talk. They effectively set the expectations for their companies with their behavior. Leaders of highly effective teams model the behavior that they desire in their team members.

## Develop Talent

In Kristine's freshman year when The University of North Carolina was playing in a 7v7 tournament, Kristine shot the ball low and into the corner of the net to score. Coach Dorrance immediately pulled her out of the game.

Getting taken out of the game initially frustrated her since she was playing well and had just scored. But then, Dorrance pulled her to the sideline and asked her, "Did you see what you just did?" She said, "Yes, I scored." It wasn't that she had just scored, Anson emphasized to her that her choice of how she scored made all the difference. The goalkeeper had remained upright on a breakaway, so the best choice in her ball placement was low and to the corner.

Too often coaching becomes about correcting what is wrong. Anson reached Kristine with a positive analysis of her game, an acknowledgment about what was right. He recognized that she'd been playing hard and reinforced that she had done well based on her competitor's position, and praised her. Then, he put her back in the game, with increased confidence and additional goal-scoring knowledge. This brief moment that Coach Dorrance took to develop Kristine's talent made her a better player than she had been five minutes earlier when she scored the goal.

Today, Kristine tries to emulate this approach at soccer clinics, taking care to be specific and positive when developing players' talent. Besides inspiring and setting expectations, the coach's role is to train each player through continuous feedback. This can be a mixture of encouragement, guidance, and direction—depending on what each individual needs from their coach. Yes, there are team drills for general soccer skills that everyone participates in; however, each player has specific development needs. This could be anything from passing, defense position, shooting technique, mental confidence, or something else. Some players even need new challenges, having mastered their previous skill development goal. Coaches should take all of this into account when developing their players.

## Plan for Succession

A business leader needs to coach and develop their direct reports. After all, these are the organization's future leaders, and the manager will need to align competency growth with an employee's job progression. By helping to promote direct reports to a new role or a new department, a leader benefits the broader organization. Some companies even reward leaders who coach direct reports effectively, giving a bonus if someone on their team is promoted across the career lattice to a new department.

Some companies have a culture where they don't share A-Team players across departments, because they feel their department "loses" even though the company as a whole "wins." For these companies that hoard talent, the department "silo mentality" not only limits their talent's career opportunities, it also hinders the business's possible performance. After profitability, succession planning is a leader's second most important responsibility. You have to prepare future leaders.

# Prepare for the Path

Employees are increasingly more focused on the learning and growth opportunities that a company offers. Yet only a few organizations look to develop individual performance through an Individual Development Plan that considers additional training, new job responsibilities, and other career development activities for that employee to grow professionally. Those that do, chart an employee's learning in order to advance their careers.

Overall, a leader is there to continuously enhance each team member's skills over time. The leader identifies the required skills for a team member's role to assess if there is a capability gap. The coaching can be tactical, where they are teaching specific skills needed to do a job more effectively. It could also be more mental, where they demonstrate how to operate as a leader in a humble yet confident manner. Coaching could also be positional, such as showing the individual how to take a long-term view of their career and to prepare so that they can be "in the right place at the right time."

The key here is that as a leader, you look to what each team member needs and customize your development of them to those specific needs to improve capabilities and address skill gaps. Like Coach Dorrance did with Kristine, it is also about being aware of teachable moments to build team members' tactical, mental, or positional skills. You'll need to balance stretching the team member's abilities with creating risk for the team. Through this professional development, the team member's engagement, motivation, and job satisfaction increase. It is about preparing the team member for the path, not preparing the path for the team member.

# Grow through Delegation

Most jobs require developing relationships and working with others. Teams are there to execute the leader's strategy. In turn, a leader must learn to delegate to the team; otherwise, the team's performance is contained to his/her individual bandwidth. If a leader tries to be the Lone Ranger, the team will be restricted. For example, if the leader is strong with administrative skills yet not relational, then they will reach their limit quickly. When this is the case, management will have to clean up the mess that a nonrelational team leader causes. Thus, it is advantageous to coach and develop team leaders to develop their connection with their colleagues.

Another aspect of delegating is taking a teamwide approach. In order to ensure that everyone has critical skill sets, strive to cross-train team members. This not only mitigates risk if a team member is not able to perform their job, it also gives another team member an opportunity to grow and develop relationships with other team members. This cross-training could be a tool for succession planning and building your talent pipeline. For the business, this reduces bottlenecks and mitigates overdependence on one key team member.

In order for a powerhouse to set the foundation, you will need a strong leader like Coach Dorrance. In the interview that follows, you will learn more about how Coach Dorrance applied these principles to literally create his very own world champion team.

## 1:1 with Coach Anson Dorrance

Coach Dorrance is one of the most successful coaches in any sport. His teams have won 90 percent of his games, and he won his 1,000th game in 2018. He has won twenty-one NCAA Women's Soccer Championships at The University of North Carolina (about ⅔ of the championships). Thirteen of his players have won twenty National Player of the Year awards. In addition, he coached the USWNT between 1986 and 1994. He was inducted into the National Soccer Hall of Fame in 2008.

### How does a coach inspire his team?

A coach has to walk his talk. When I began coaching professional women's soccer, I was excited about the future of the women's game, to the extent that I just wanted to be an equipment manager for the first World Cup in China. However, I ended up being coach. When we traveled to China, we rode a coal train from the airport to the hotel, having to dust ourselves off when we arrived. I remember the sheets were so grimy that we all wore our clothes to bed. We did not complain about a thing. Whining was not allowed.

We were selling the game, showing how women could play, and telling the world that the women's game was worth watching. Yes, we had to deal with all the adversities that selling the women's game would entail. It was beyond the individual for the growth of the game, which required personal humility and character. Everyone played for each other, and we got to live a dream. Isn't that incredible?

## How do you effectively set team expectations?

At The University of North Carolina, freshman players are stepping into something great, something bigger than themselves when they first arrive on campus. We have a deep culture that begins before they ever step on the field. For example, we have a book club where we meet weekly to discuss the book, its topic, and how it relates to team members as a player and as a person. Through this, new players learn about the goals we have for them, which extend well beyond the athletic department. These books range from popular business books, to books written by alumni soccer players, to books written by professors. You are the foreman of your own construction project, and to get to your potential, you need to learn what extraordinary people have done.

When I look at the USWNT, it is about the people you gather together and their character. Kristine was gritty. She was off the charts. I can still see her drive during one of our alumni soccer games at UNC! Michelle Akers was killing herself to win games, and that becomes a part of your culture. Time and time again, we praised character and effort instead of talent. The culture is built on the character traits of those on the roster. We praised the right attitude, the effort, and the human character in the most positive sense. After every practice, we talked about positive aspects of what we were seeing by naming names.

## As coach, how do you develop talent?

I look at a player's athletic character, which is comprised of self-discipline, competitive fire, self-belief, grit, love of playing the game, and some other factors. To get a player to reach her full potential, they have to understand their own internal narrative. This is designed to protect you, as the weaker you are, the more excuses you build to protect you when you fail. You can't be afraid of failure. You have to be responsible for it.

As their coach, I help players break down their internal narrative so they own everything they are achieving and not achieving. When we meet during a personal conference, I attempt to get their internal narrative close to the truth so they can improve. They have to make the decision on if they are going to get to their potential. Does this player decide to become her best?

Many talented players do not make that decision and are full of excuses for not taking responsibility. However, during my player conference with one player, I asked her flat out, "What do you want to do?" She said, "I want to be the best in the world." Ecstatic with her response, I got up and turned the light switch off and then on, showing her that she had just flipped the switch. We then had the conversation that if she had decided to become the best in the world, this is what has to happen. I'm happy to report that this player was Mia Hamm, and she definitely did it!

## Tactics for Your Team

A powerhouse sets the foundation with a leader who inspires, sets expectations, and develops talent. Leaders inspire by motivating the team to be ready to sacrifice so the team as a whole can succeed. They also set expectations by helping teams gain clarity on what is expected from each member on the team while setting boundaries on behavior. And last, leaders develop talent by helping team members improve their knowledge, skills, and abilities through career development opportunities.

Consider the following. At your organization, how will you:

1. Motivate team members to work hard to contribute?

2. Provide clear-cut and specific agreements around team norms required for acceptable conduct?

3. Initiate learning opportunities for personal growth and improvement leading to career development?

*Carla Overbeck and Kristine celebrate around the field in Landover after beating Germany in the World Cup quarterfinals on July 1, 1999. They won 3–2, and Kristine claims, "It was one of the most up and down games I was ever a part of. A game that dealt with some adversity and lots of celebration." (Credit: Pam Whitesell/ isiphotos.com)*

# Leading the Team

*"You must be able to put all*
*individual goals and achievements aside*
*for the betterment of the team."*

—**Carla Overbeck**

A good leader is required for good teamwork, both on and off the field. Kristine enjoyed being her soccer team captain. She was the captain at Wilton High School her junior and senior years. She also served as captain at UNC in her sophomore and senior year and then again for the USWNT from 2005–2007. She also served as captain for her professional team, the Boston Breakers, in both leagues, the WUSA and the WPS (Women's Professional Soccer).

As captain, she was constantly trying to connect with the players. She wanted to make sure they all felt she was approachable and was there for them. As captain, she continuously reached out to engage each teammate.

She did this by eating with different team members at meals, warming up with different players, and sitting next to different teammates on the bus. Kristine felt it was just as important to connect with the players off the field as much as it was to jell with them on the field. Every little thing mattered, and she knew that from experiences she had being led by other captains. These small moments of interaction from a captain helped motivate a team.

A captain is the leader of the team who connects and builds trust among the team members. They are the voice of the players, and they share feedback from the players to the coach. They have the opportunity to build a tight-knit team or a frayed one. Often soccer teams have co-captains who share the responsibilities. Julie Foudy and Carla Overbeck were two of the best captains of the USWNT. Their ability to get the best out of their teammates was powerful. They did it with love, passion, laughter, and honesty.

Playing on many teams through the years, Kristine got to see different styles of leadership from different captains. For the USWNT, Julie Foudy was passionate and vocal. Joy Fawcett led by example, and Carla Overbeck was balanced and reinforcing. They were remarkable captains, all different yet effective with their own leadership attributes, which enabled them to bring out the best in their team. Each captain needed different skills and objectives to be effective for different teams and different situations. This is the same in the corporate world, where business leaders build team commitment and confidence to drive superior performance.

## Why Leading Is Important

Situational leadership is being able to adjust your leadership approach to a specific situation. This could be establishing a new team by selecting team members, aligning the team direction, or collaborating on the team's execution. Or, it could be that the team leader needs to turn around a broken team by implementing new processes, energizing low-morale team members, and ensuring deliverable timelines are met. Another situation may be taking over the big shoes of a high-performing team, and the team leader needs to build team members' trust by making good decisions. Essentially, a company needs a leader who can improve team dynamics contingent on the situation.

It is important to note that each leader serves under similar and different situations, just like a corporate leader is under the influence of organizational conditions. For the USWNT, it was the coach, the expectations for the team to win, and their previous performance outcome (e.g., did they win the previous World Cup/Olympics). For corporate leaders, this could be situational differences such as management practices, working conditions, the perception of members, and the characteristics of tasks.

The team leader's role definitely has an impact on the team's effectiveness, specifically when it comes to such things as asserting authority, informal authority, and aligning incentives.

## Assert Authority

A team leader needs to assert authority. Players are peers. Yes, there are differentiators among them, such as tenure on the team, skill/proficiency levels, position, and playing time. A team's captain is granted some degree of formal authority by her peers. The new captain always has "shoes to fill," so the largest challenge for a new captain is learning how to fill her own cleats. The team looks to the captain to set the example for the team, to be a positive influence, and to never show defeat. When team members observe the captain, they learn what their team culture is. A captain models work ethic and respect in how they train and how they treat every individual on the team.

In contrast, a coach once assigned two captains for a team who were not the players the team members would have chosen. One was not liked and the other was not noticed. The team did not respond to these captains because they did not have respect for them, and this hurt the team's effectiveness.

Kristine strived to lead like her fantastic predecessors when she was captain of the USWNT. Her personal style of leadership was more "lead by example." Everything that she asked her teammates to do, she made sure that she did first. For example, fitness was critical for their team's success. She was always at the top of the fitness standards, and she let her work ethic and commitment be an example for her teammates.

## Command Respect

For business professionals, a leader's peers are colleagues with differentiators such as their tenure with the company, years of experience, and education level. A business leader may have formal authority with a title like manager or supervisor, or informal authority where they do not have a title yet hold influence over the group. This leader, working within a formal as well as informal social structure, sets the tone for how team members will work together, communicate, collaborate, trust, manage conflict, and perform.

You do not want to be known as a leader who "kisses up and kicks down." Like the earlier story about a coach assigning the wrong players to be the team captains, if a company assigns a supervisor who does not command the respect of the team, then the business team's effectiveness decreases. A leader should garner respect, assert authority, and set the team culture so they can become a high-performing team.

Sometimes, a peer becomes a leader when they are promoted to a management role over previous peers. How this newly promoted leader asserts authority will have an overall impact on their effectiveness. As an example, as one individual contributor moved into her first leadership role, she was replacing a successful and well-liked leader. She knew it would be a challenge to fill his shoes. On her first day of the job, a respected organizational leader came into her new office and nonchalantly said, "It is your time to shine, not to reflect." With this simple statement, he helped her realize that she needed to pave her own path, instead of trying to portray the image of her predecessor.

## Collaborative Leadership

Each leader will bring his or her unique style. A leader influences team members' attitude and work. The leader is conversely affected by the other members of the team. It is important there be a match between the leader's style of interaction with the members and the degree to which the situation gives control and influence to the leader. This team-leader fit helps leadership provide what the team members need.

It is the team that determines what types of authority they will support from the leader. How a leader asserts her authority is a key factor for the team members who follow her. When she asserts her authority appropriately, the leader will become an effective collaborator with the team. A democratic leadership style that encourages the team members to collaborate with their leader should empower the team members while expecting them to respectfully defer to the leader when necessary for team alignment. The leader would gently lead her team, advocating for particular decisions, actively supporting or opposing others' recommendations, training team members, and engaging in consensus building and compromise. This type of leader makes sure all team members are "part of the circle" and feel like equals.

Yet, the leader still needs to assert authority. If they go too far in being open to new ideas, it's not healthy for the team. Team members do not want a leader whose behavior is overly passive and who unquestioningly goes along with others' decisions. If he does not assert his authority correctly, he will not be able to collaborate effectively.

The opposite of this collaborative, democratic style of leadership is an authoritative one where team members feel controlled. This kind of leader may give too much direction. Team members do not want a domineering leader who tries to control everything. The key is for the leader to strike a good balance between collaboration and asserting authority, because too much authoritative style will negatively affect team performance.

## Competence and Character

Much of a leader's success in their role comes down to the leader's competence and character. One university president found that out of all leadership traits, followers needed to believe that a leader was competent at making healthy decisions to sustain and grow their organization.

A competent leader needs to juggle many factors while making decisions. They have multiple stakeholders to be accountable to—the team, customers, and more. Each group has their own requests of the leader, which can distract them from the actual team. A competent leader is able to balance board pressure, financial distress, hiring, and other factors without taking their eye off the ball.

People also want to follow a leader that they believe is going to do the right thing, especially during stressful or challenging situations. This goodwill speaks to their leader's character. Teams more easily place their trust in a leader who demonstrates the authenticity, integrity, and ability to make the correct decisions for the organization.

## Lead Informally

When Kristine didn't serve as team captain, her role was to follow the teammate who had been selected to lead. This following of the leader is still a leadership role; it just doesn't come with a title. You could say it is a role of informal authority. It is more pull than push. It is setting the example for the team, showing up the way you want others to show up.

In soccer, the team captain wears the arm band that designates she has the formal leadership role, but players like Michelle Akers, Mia Hamm, and Abby Wambach rarely wore the arm band. They didn't have to, as they had a presence when they stepped on the field, and they were going to score goals and follow their captain to ensure that happened. They had reputational authority and didn't need an arm band, as the other players wanted to support them to make them successful because they were playing for the good of the team. These informal leaders created energy and enthusiasm that was contagious for the entire team.

Kristine remembers experiences like these fondly. "When Mia would get in her moment and be on fire, you would listen. When Michelle was speaking with her years of experience, you would listen. And when Abby got all fired up, you'd laugh a bit because she was so passionate and loud, but then you would always follow her." These leaders with informal authority were on a mission, and the team eagerly followed their example.

## Recognize Informal Leaders

Not everyone can be the leader. You have to know when to lead, when to follow, when to support, and when to get out of a leader's way.

It is much easier to lead when supported. It is a lonely feeling when you are striking out by yourself without that immediate support system of others on your team to help you bring strength to the team. There are many famous "leaders" in history who did not have a specific leadership title. For example, Martin Luther King Jr. was a pastor, and Gandhi was a lawyer. Yet, they had informal authority, as they are famous for roles for which there was not an official promotion to a specific title.

As a team member, you need to know when a team needs you to lead and when the team needs you to follow. If everyone tries to lead, then there are "too many cooks in the kitchen," leading to poor performance. If you are leading, then remember to empower and recognize those supportive followers who are aligned to the team's direction. If you are following, then remember to support your leader by executing the communicated game plan.

# Align Incentives

It's crucial for a leader to align incentives to affirm team members' contributions to the team goals. Assess and reward an individual's contribution to the team, such as collaboration. When the team goals direct the team member's individual goals, it is called cascading goals and is typically handled through the annual performance review process. When a company rewards the team for accomplishing their collective goal, this helps eliminate "hidden agendas," "power plays," "competing agendas," and the "empire building" that hurt so many teams today.

For example, one civilian foreign intelligence service is tasked with the job of gathering, processing, and analyzing national security information from around the world. Case officers are evaluated on two separate metrics: recruiting "targets" and obtaining human intelligence. However, the bureaucracy evaluates individuals instead of the team. Thus, it creates a competitive, cut-throat environment between case officers where one's success is detracting to another's work. The case officers were constantly worried that other case officers were doing better, as each was out on their own. If they had instead emphasized the accomplishments of the team, there would have been more incentive to work together, resulting in more trust and care among the group. They would have also recruited more spies, their primary objective, because they could have optimized the matching of case officers with targets. In these ever-changing political, social, economic, technological, and military landscapes, we need to align our team incentives so that we can improve our intelligence gathering.

# Extrinsic Motivation

From an extrinsic motivation perspective, the gold medal or world championship drives soccer players while they train. When the team won, they realized all their hard work paid off. If they did not win, then they would reassess what they could have done different during the preparation and practice that would have made their performance better.

Extrinsic motivation is when you try to motivate a team member by providing them a goal, tangible reward, or pressure. Once they achieve their goal, you could use external motivation by providing an incentive to encourage ongoing performance. This award could be winning a contest, getting a job promotion, increasing responsibility, receiving recognition at work, or getting a financial bonus in your paycheck. This milestone celebration of the "win" positively affects momentum. Typically, this has a short-term impact on the team. The challenge is that extrinsic motivation must be consistently renewed.

In a transactional work environment, there is a reciprocal agreement between company and employee: salary and recognition are given in exchange for effort. In a transformational work environment, management is not a "command and control" that strictly monitors employees. Instead, it rewards employees for greater effort and team cohesion.

## Intrinsic Motivation

Another approach you could take with your team is to use intrinsic motivation. Belonging to the team after going through tryouts encourages the team member's efforts. Leaders create that meaning from being on a team to work together to accomplish their collective purpose. That intrinsically motivates.

These motivations are not tangible things like awards or raises, but internal desires such as job satisfaction, a sense of meaning, and belonging. These motivations have a greater long-term impact on the team. Leaders should affirm the contribution and can publicly praise the well-regarded individual or team. Often.

A team example of intrinsic motivation is a nonprofit board of directors. They are not paid, nor do they spend much time together. However, their teamwork is critical to the organization's health, as they often have fiduciary and governance responsibility. Thus, they need to have excellent teamwork with minimal time spent together and no financial incentive. Their incentive is intrinsic, the sustainability and impact of the nonprofit accomplishing its mission. This intrinsic motivation rewards the nonprofit board members because they enjoy serving on the board and believe that the fulfillment of the mission will have positive impacts on the community.

A powerhouse needs a leader to assert authority, as well as informal leaders to take their supportive role. They also need a reward system based on the individual's contribution to the team. In the interview that follows, you will learn how Carla Overbeck captained the USWNT using the principles of asserting authority, informal authority, and aligning incentives.

# 1:1 with Carla Overbeck

Carla Overbeck was captain of the USWNT from 1995 to 2000. When Kristine became the team captain later, she would call Carla for mentoring advice. When Carla played at UNC, she did not lose one of her ninety-five games over four years. She was inducted in the National Soccer Hall of Fame in 2006. Today, she is an assistant coach for Duke University's women's soccer team, where she has been for over twenty years.

## How did you assert authority as captain for the USWNT?

Once I became captain, I felt a responsibility to do the right thing. Being the captain of a team like this is quite an honor, and I did not want to let people down. I wanted to be the best I could be for the team and spend energy on what the team needed. I wanted to live up to the honor of being their leader.

My job was easy because the nature of the personalities of the veteran players on the team. I intentionally got to know people off the field, where I did not take myself seriously and was funny. Yet, on the field, I was all business. If you know them off the field, then they work hard for you on the field.

Our whole team was based on servant leadership—wanting to serve your teammates. I would get off the bus and grab the ball bag, because it was the right thing to do. The equipment manager should not have to carry all the large bags. I was no better than anyone else on the team just because I was captain, so why would I walk by the ball bag and not pick it up? Everyone on a team helps and contributes. It's important to ask yourself what you can bring to a team; I brought a good work ethic.

As captain, I did not let anything slip away, so I had difficult conversations with people who were going off track to remind them what the team's goals were. No one wants to be humiliated in front of the whole group. Instead, I pulled the individual aside and encouraged them in a nice and genuine way. They knew the high standard I held for myself, and because of that I could get onto the superstars and tell them what they weren't doing right on the field. Everyone—the starters and the reserves—was treated equally. Team members respected me as captain so I was able to get on them when they did something wrong. They wanted to know so they could fix it and improve. Everyone likes positivity, so I tried to find something they did well and told them that, too. When they did well, I was all over them with praise!

## Why is informal authority important to effective teamwork?

All team members are called to do the right thing, which means putting your personal agenda aside. For the USWNT, it is not about how many goals you score or how many times you are in the paper or how many awards you win, because you wouldn't be anything without the team. You should deflect attention to the team like Mia Hamm did. When she was the face of women's soccer, she tirelessly promoted being a member of our team. It wasn't about her.

You can tell when people are having bad days and help turn it around, if you have a sense of what is going on in the team. For example, if Kristine was slacking off, I would be positive with encouragement, saying, "Hey, Kristine Lilly, we need you!" Tone is the most important thing, as I have been on teams where there are screamers who are negative. I didn't want to be like that. I wanted to be positive to get the most out of people and to be helpful.

## How did the incentives align with your individual and team goals?

When I got to UNC and played for Anson, initially I was afraid of being too competitive. They'd lost the national championship the year before I got there, and all the defense players graduated. I was homesick and I wanted everyone to like me. I thought I would not have friends if I won the competitions. When I went into "the hut," where each team member's performance was ranked, I was at the bottom of the 1v1 ladder.

Over the next four years, I worked hard and matured. I realized we were all on the same page and wanted to win and that it's OK to compete. We were all trying to win, and this made everyone better—including me. I rose toward the top of the 1v1 ranking. The competitive environment and posting of goals set the standard for the incoming players, establishing our team value system.

Our team had so many talented players. We knew that the person next to us had a special talent, and to put those all together would make us a pretty successful team. However, you must be able to put all your individual goals and achievements aside for the betterment of the team.

## Tactics for Your Team

It's important that leaders assert authority so that you lead your powerhouse in a manner that matches your level of control to the situation. You also want to recognize and encourage informal leaders who influence and affect the team even though they do not have an official leader title. Finally, you should motivate your team members to recognize their contributions to the team, not just individual performance.

Consider applying these three principles to your own organization. How will you:

1. Lead with an interactive style that matches the situation requirements for level of control?

2. Recognize leaders without titles who influence and affect the team in a positive way?

3. Reward performance based on team collaboration and achievement?

*Kristine stands in the Chinese wall, ready to disrupt their defense during the final of the 1999 World Cup. "When I look back at this photo I can feel the heat of that day and the intensity of that game," Kristine said. "The game ended 0–0 and went to penalty kicks that we won 5–4. One of the greatest days of my life." (Credit: John Todd/isiphotos.com)*

# Serving on International Teams

*"Sport unites; we don't believe it should separate."*[23]

**—adidas CEO Kasper Rørsted**

During Kristine's career, she went to China over ten times. In the late '80s and early '90s the Chinese were enthralled with the USWNT. In the beginning it wasn't necessarily about the soccer, but more so about seeing Americans. They were intrigued by the cultural differences. The players, too, were intrigued by China's culture and infrastructure, specifically their transportation system, which relied heavily on bicycles. When the USWNT won the 1991 World Cup over the Chinese home team, Chinese fans chased after the team's bus to get autographs. They likely did not know the players' names, but they wanted a player card. The USWNT players handed the cards out the window of the bus to the fans. Cultural differences disappeared between them in moments like these: they were fans who loved soccer and loved the USWNT.

Kristine and her teammates helped establish women's soccer worldwide. She competed in five FIFA World Cups around the globe, playing in twenty-one

23 Peter Verry, "Adidas CEO Kasper Rørsted on How Kanye West's Politics Have Affected the Brand," Footwear News.com, November 6, 2018, https://footwearnews.com/2018/influencers/power-players/adidas-ceo-rorsted-interview-sales-kanye-west-1202703494/.

countries against thirty-nine different teams. They went to China in 1991, Sweden in 1995, and back to China in 2007. Two of her Olympics included Australia in 2000 and Greece in 2004. During those forty-six matches in eight global tournaments, their high-performing team had thirty-nine wins, three losses, and four draws. Kristine and her teammates thoroughly enjoyed the opportunity to be on the global stage—interacting with soccer players from all over the world. Today the National Women's Soccer League (NWSL) has players from many countries. With global teammates who are playing soccer together, there is an even greater need to create a high-performing team in order to win on the field.

Kristine also played professionally overseas and saw firsthand how cultural differences can play out on the soccer field. When the WUSA professional league terminated, Kristine left the States to play for the Swedish club KIF Örebro DFF in 2005. When Kristine played in Sweden, some aspects of training sessions differed from what she was used to in the US. For example, during drills if the ball went out of bounds, the Swedish team would play on and disregard the boundaries. This was different than in the US, where drills had boundaries that players stayed between, represented by the lines or cones on the field. In order to thrive in this new environment, Kristine had to adapt to the Swedish rules of play.

## Why Global Teams Are Important

Soccer has an international influence, as do multinational companies. The people coming together on teams in these organizations are often from different locations and cultures. Corporations are not only more diverse in their makeup but also in the markets they are operating in. Many organizations need to have cross-cultural appeal for their products and services as companies look to diversify their market footprint. Yet, global organizations cannot offer an "off-the-shelf" team approach. Instead, they must consider the culture, customs, and laws in each country.

Many core aspects of a team and its culture will shift depending on the people who are working together: how a team communicates, what technology is available, and the amount of compensation will all differ between regions. Research has shown that teams mixed by country of origin were more likely to experience conflict due to the language barriers and cultural differences. In order to be effective, teams in different places need to be cognizant of local practices so they can adapt.[24] This sort of teamwork can be accomplished by being culturally aware, cross-pollinating ideas, and dispersing digital tools.

## Women's Sports and Social Equality

Women's soccer is a guiding indicator of a woman's ability to realize her potential in different societies. Women's international soccer is affected by each country's economic wealth and level of gender equality.

While men's soccer is a sport for the masses, it appears that a country's wealth predicts the success of women's soccer. Wealthy countries like the USA and China, for example, provide a highly organized sporting activity in school or government settings. Their national wealth provides funds to invest in women's sports. When you historically analyze the top performing teams, they primarily come from countries with market-based and commercially oriented countries, such as Australia, Brazil, Canada, Denmark, England, France, Germany, Italy, Japan, New Zealand, Norway, Scotland, South Korea, Spain, and Switzerland.

Success in women's sports reveals the level of gender inequality per country. A country's gender inequality negatively affects their women's soccer team performance. This inequality can be measured using the ratio of women's earnings to men's earnings, as well as the Gender-Related Development Index (GDI) compiled by the United Nations Development Program. In Latin American countries, for example, gender roles and the society's elevation of masculinity negatively affect the number of women playing soccer.[25]

---

24  Xusen Cheng, Guopeng Yin, Aida Azadegan, and Gwendolyn Kolfschoten, "Trust Evolvement in Hybrid Team Collaboration: A Longitudinal Case Study," *Group Decision and Negotiation* 25, no. 2 (May 2015), https://www.researchgate.net/publication/277352784_Trust_Evolvement_in_Hybrid_Team_Collaboration_A_Longitudinal_Case_Study.

25  Robert Hoffmann, Lee Chew Ging, Victor Matheson, and Bala Ramasamy, "International Women's Football and Gender Inequality," *Applied Economics Letters* 13, no. 15 (December 2006): 999–1001, https://www.researchgate.net/publication/233052443_International_women's_football_and_gender_inequality#39;s_football_and_gender_inequality.

# Be Culturally Aware

As companies go global, they must consider where to expand. Factors such as economic wealth, political systems, and gender equality are only a few of the considerations that companies should take into account when looking to increase their company's reach. Integration responsibilities, national boundaries, cultural diversity, local responsiveness, evolving business environments, and different cultural norms and values will also affect the cross-cultural awareness needed to make effective business decisions.

For example, companies often perform geopolitical research to determine the level of risks that an investment holds in certain countries or areas. While the business case for such expansion may indicate the potential substantial revenue and profit, there may be a degree of risk that deters the organization from making the investment. The same is true for the degree of complexity that investing in business in another country holds. Sometimes the costs, risks, or uncertainties outweigh the known substantial benefits. Thus, a company's risk aversion prevents them from global expansion in specific areas of the world. While a company's global team will have standardized expertise, the local team will have insight into the country's culture, opportunities, and threats and can help the organization adapt accordingly.

## Variances in Teamwork

As a business expands into new areas, leaders should be aware of how definitions of teamwork vary across cultural contexts. Although the team roles, scope, and goals remain the same, the preferred teamwork practices may be different based on national cultures. The underlying cultural value variation affects different social behaviors, such as leadership, decision making, aggression, conflict resolution, and conformity. These are different expectations on how the team will be managed and how it will operate. As a result, a multinational team operating with many cultures will have to adapt to team members having different teamwork expectations.

An example of a team dealing with different cultural expectations was a global technology implementation. While the company headquarters were in Canada where the implementation team operated, the deployment phases went around the globe. This global team had to adapt to local preferences in order to be successful. In Great Britain, this meant small differences like the size of standard paper in the printer or the preference of a rain coat for team swag (useful for their weather) instead of the usual company-issued hoodie (which was culturally looked down upon). In Asia, the attempt to survey employees for input had minimal impact due to their hesitation to give feedback. In South America, meetings always started late even though timing was critical to the team. The company's financial cost grew the longer the project ran, yet in Europe no one works in August and the organization burned millions while the local employees took their annual vacation. The team adapted to each local variation in order to overcome the differences and implement the technology on budget and on time.

## Cross-Pollinate

While the term "cross-pollination" originally came about to describe the process of plants fertilizing each other with pollen, it has evolved to encompass the sharing of ideas between cultures. Essentially, it is taking what is good from a country and adapting it to another area, like Tex-Mex food coming from Mexico and now being a staple of Texas cuisine.

Soccer, as the most popular sport in the world, provides a platform for cross-pollination.

Philippe Troussier, a Frenchman who coached the Japanese National team for four years, was able to take expertise from France's soccer world and make it successful in Japan's sport culture.[26]

Japan hosted the World Cup in 2002, even though they had never won a single game in the World Cup prior. A culture full of national pride, they did not want to be humiliated at home. They surprised many when they deviated from their tradition and hired an outsider, rather than someone from within their country and the known pool of resources.

In Japan, leaders like CEOs and head coaches have long been chosen from inside an organization, rather than externally. The leader is often close to the team members in the business and is comfortable with the established working practices. The new leader typically does not make large changes, as there is a focus on continuity instead of large reforms. This practice stems

26  Risaburo Nezu, "Japan: In Search of a Winning Formula," *OECD Observer* 234 (October 2002).

from the fear that a major change from the way things are done would result in confusion and create a loss of loyalty and decreased morale.

For this World Cup, when Japan selected Coach Troussier, many doubted the wisdom of this decision and were suspicious. Troussier did not speak a word of Japanese and had to use an interpreter to communicate with his players. The language barrier was minimal when you consider the many other ways that Troussier's appointment was counter to Japanese culture.

First, the Japanese sports community recognizes collective achievement over individual successes. Troussier countered that by increasing competition among teammates, similar to what Coach Dorrance cultivated at his soccer team's practices.

Second, Troussier created a public uproar when he did not choose the popular players with seniority for the final team. Instead, he chose several good younger players with international potential who had previously not been given the chance to demonstrate their talents on the world stage. This approach may sound familiar to what Coach Dorrance did when he selected Kristine and other teenagers to join the USWNT and play in China for the 1991 World Cup.

Third, Troussier countered the more polite and passive Japanese culture by asking for more aggression on the soccer field. When frustrated, he criticized Japanese attitudes on the soccer field, saying, "Those who wait until the traffic signal turns green are of no use on the pitch. You must go when there is no car coming."

Fourth, Troussier also countered Japan's more silent and evasive management culture by being open and transparent, which was quite a sharp contrast to what the team was accustomed to. He told the team what his expectations were and the role that he wanted for the team. In addition to him being open with the team, he also asked his players to be open and transparent with him. He urged them to come forward and speak clearly, as opposed to their culture that complies with authority by not overtly sharing thoughts or opinions.

By allowing for cross-pollination and hiring a foreign coach to lead Japan's soccer team, the team got exposed to a new style and approach to the game. This cross-pollination ended up working in their favor, as the Japanese team won games and made it to World Cup group play. Coach Troussier has since become a national hero. Despite the initial controversy and resistance to his new tactics, he now enjoys widespread respect in Japan. If

Japan had hired someone from within their country, they most likely would have not made the large changes that were needed by the soccer program to be successful.

## Share Better Practices

Many businesses are also going global and embracing team cross-pollination. Like Troussier, many leaders are crossing borders to rescue troubled companies. Linguistic, cultural, political, economic, and social borders are coming down. Outsourcing and offshoring continue to shrink the globe. Global trade and international investments are on the rise.

To successfully compete in this international market, companies must continue to find ways to encourage team cross-pollination. This includes looking externally and globally for leadership by fundamentally altering existing operations instead of relying on continuity. This new approach requires an increased awareness of cultural differences and a willingness to abandon the status quo. Those companies who cannot find leaders who are prepared to lead globally will not be as successful as those companies that implement the strategy of cross-pollination.

For example, many corner offices in the United States are filled with foreign-born leaders, and not ones only from Canada or Europe anymore; they come from diverse and far-flung countries such as India and Russia. As companies look to expand globally for revenue, it only makes sense that they would acquire leadership talent globally also.

## Utilize Digital Teams

In the beginning, the USWNT did not get together very often to train, only two to three times a year. When Kristine was not practicing with the USWNT, she had to train on her own. She had to be fit and "played in," which means running, getting touches on the ball, and finding someone to work with to be "game ready."

Kristine and her teammates had to find ways to be ready so that they could contribute to the team. Coaches set the expectations, yet it was up to the individual to honor their responsibility to do their own work. So Kristine and her team members would call each other to see what they were doing for workouts and hold each other accountable. They were responsible for their commitment to be ready when called upon. Those who were not game ready when the team did get together ended up being left behind by not starting or not being asked back onto the team. The players had to continue to perform on their own in order to help the team be successful when they got called in. The success that the team experienced created a sense of responsibility the players felt for each other and the game.

## Remote Teams

Giving remote workers clear expectations and the ability to connect with each other is crucial to the success of a remote team. As more companies take global initiatives like strategic partnering, they need global teams who work across time, organizational boundaries, and geographical boundaries. For companies, there is a cost savings opportunity when teams work virtually, in the form of reduced travel costs and employees being located where the cost of living is cheaper. In addition, there is an efficiency play by leveraging time zone differences so work can happen 24/7. A team can balance global and local knowledge, combining the standardized competencies and processes with insights about the specific countries.

## Digital Tools for Dispersed Teams

Even when work is done remotely, a team member needs to interact to understand her contribution to the team's goals. A phrase heard often is, "Teamwork doesn't tolerate the inconvenience of distance."

However, these new global teams bring with them new challenges, as logistics become much more difficult, given dissimilarities in available resources, accents, culture, customs, compensation, and other regional factors. Research shows that less face-to-face interaction results in greater distrust and information hoarding, unwillingness to take risks and learn from mistakes, and even inaction and team paralysis. Geographic dispersion may impede effective information sharing, coordination, problem solving, and trust building. This dispersion also hinders the ability to constructively resolve conflicts with far-flung members of the team. These challenges can be expected to intensify as the level of team dispersion increases.[27]

To counter this, the team needs to interact in a highly supportive, frequent, and responsive manner to build task-based trust. Digital tools can be an instrumental resource for these situations. For example, web conference tools enable team members in different parts of the globe to see each other's body language during a virtual team meeting. This creates a face-to-face dynamic even when working together from a great distance. On the flip side, a team member's comfort level with the electronic communication technology determines if it is a smooth or turbulent experience. Teamwork quality and computer self-efficacy significantly and positively improve electronic communications. This results in a significant and positive impact on team performance, even if they never meet face-to-face.

## Bridge Boundaries

Leaders need to recognize and bridge the boundaries that may cause differences in team member perspectives and work approaches. Virtual teams can present a challenge as classic face-to-face collaboration is compromised. Team collaboration and the willingness to share knowledge are linked to the presence of trust. This virtual and dispersed work environment requires a different type of leader who can lead by example. The virtual leader should be able to coach and display empathy when not face-to-face with others on the team. With teams that operate in a global work environment, a dispersed team needs an empowering leader to delegate responsibilities to the team members. When a leader does delegate responsibility to his or her team, this raises the team members' level of intrinsic motivation and participative decision making. This leader's approach should facilitate, support, and promote virtual collaboration. When done well, this will contribute to high levels of team performance.[28]

---

27  N. Sharon Hill and Kathryn M. Bartol, "Empowering Leadership and Effective Collaboration in Geographically Dispersed Teams," *Personnel Psychology* 69, no. 1 (Spring 2016): 159–98.

28  N. Sharon Hill and Kathryn M. Bartol, "Empowering Leadership and Effective Collaboration in Geographically Dispersed Teams," *Personnel Psychology* 69, no. 1 (Spring 2016): 159–98.

In order for a powerhouse to achieve the tactic of serving on international teams, it needs to be culturally aware, cross-pollinate, and use digital tools when dispersed. In the interview that follows, you will learn more about how adidas applies these principles as a successful international company.

# 1:1 with adidas®

Multinational sportswear manufacturer corporation adidas is Kristine's long-time sponsor. She filmed the commercial "Impossible is Nothing" for them. Known as the "three stripes company" because of their logo, adidas operates globally from their headquarters in Germany. Chris McGuire, a sports marketing leader, shares how the adidas teams operate internationally.

## While expanding your global footprint, how is adidas culturally aware to locals?

We have sales launch activations at various venues in partnership with local communities around the world. This is to increase brand desirability, by building our global brand in global cities like Los Angeles, New York, London, Paris, Shanghai, and Tokyo.

adidas also has a social purpose to connect locally, as we can change lives through sport. Through our "month of purpose," we intentionally volunteer through community service initiatives to provide underserved kids access to sports, helping them overcome hurdles along the way. In addition, we partnered to build fifty soccer pitches in New York City and provide children programs that promote healthy eating habits, active living, and mentorship. Finally, we have also focused on the environment by making jerseys for Major League Soccer (MLS) and University of Miami football jerseys out of recycled materials.

## How does adidas effectively cross-pollinate better practices across boundaries?

Our network of the CLG (Core Leadership Group) as well as the ELG (Extended Leadership Group) gather in regular meetings to hear, discuss, ideate, and plan for the future of the brand across the globe. In addition, our GHIPO (Global High Potential group), a team of select high-performing individuals from each market and global group, comes together to learn about key issues and opportunities, and to provide input on potential solutions. We have a Global Talent Carousel (rotation of function, culture, and location) where talented individuals move throughout the organization in a twelve-month rotation to get a good flavor of new markets, cultures, and functions.

### Because the adidas workforce is dispersed globally, how do you leverage digital technology to build teams and facilitate teamwork?

We are a global company with multiple cultures, time zones, and languages. Our company hosts private and public workspaces so employees can manage projects, share information, and ensure information is available to those who both want and need it. We use digital tools to connect us all together, including:

- company intranet to help share ideas around the globe
- video streaming and recordings to ensure key information from leadership is never missed
- web-enabled conference solutions allow us to meet without geographical limitations, in both small (1:1) and large (hundreds) groups

## Tactics for Your Team

When serving on international teams, be culturally aware, as your culture's norms and expectations are different than others. You also want to cross-pollinate, in order to learn about better practices from other countries that you can adopt and bring back to your business. And, finally, your dispersed teams should go digital to build team trust and collaboration.

Consider applying these three principles to your own organization. How will you:

1. Understand different teamwork practices across cultures?

2. Consider external better practices for internal inclusion?

3. Use digital tools to enhance virtual team members' collaboration?

# Pillar 3:

# ACHIEVE

A powerhouse achieves by learning how to be highly interactive. They accomplish this with open and effective communication resulting in productive collaboration. In addition, these teams win consistently by dedicating effort to handling team conflicts as they arise so that they do not distract from reaching their goals.

*This is a photo of David (Kristine's husband and a Brookline firefighter); Kristine's daughters, Sidney and Jordan; and Kristine at TD Bank Arena in Boston after David participated in a fund-raiser event. He climbed up hundreds of stairs in full uniform to help raise money for the American Lung Association. According to Kristine, "Not only is he everyone's hero, but also his family's hero." (Credit: The Lilly-Heavey Family)*

# Learning Teamwork

*"I have prepared myself physically and mentally*
*for any task at hand."*

—**David Heavey**

S occer is different than many other sports because it emphasizes the collective group of players over an individual athlete. In basketball there are isolation plays, baseball has individual execution, and even American football short set plays dictate exactly what a player is supposed to do.

Unlike these sports, soccer players are always interdependent on one another in a fluid, creative, and ever-changing context on the field. Players must know each other so well that they can intuitively sense what other players are going to do, as an effective team member will know where any given player is going on the field to pass the ball to them, even when they have not indicated where they are headed. What one player does on the field impacts what another does—where they move to, what the strategy is, and so forth. Once the players practice enough together to learn about each other's tendencies, then it is time to hit the field.

Kristine and some of her teammates played together for over seventeen years, creating tendencies and trust that were as natural as breathing. She knew if Mia got the ball in the attacking third of the field that she would take on the defender and go to goal. Kristine's job was to follow the play and be there for anything. Kristine knew that when she crossed the ball into the box, she trusted that Abby would be ready to head the ball into the goal. These opportunities were not chance or luck, they were teamwork cultivated over time and characterized by trust and confidence.

## Why Learning Teamwork Is Important

Knowing how to be a part of a team is a capability that a person can use in many areas of their life—sports, business, and community. Part of learning how to be on a team involves spending time with your teammates and developing the skills that you need to pull your group to succeed. Even in business, teams need to prepare and practice, as hard work precedes success when a team finally performs. During these two stages of preparation and practice, teamwork is worked on, developed, and fine-tuned.

## Prepare

The preparation stage entails an individual taking responsibility to get ready to perform their tasks physically, mentally, and emotionally. To prepare is hard work, as it involves readying, studying, thinking, and learning. The person does not wait to be assigned to a team to prepare; instead he is expanding his capabilities continuously before he joins the team. These are the team members who are willing to go the extra mile.

To be successful during each soccer match, players don't simply run out on the field. Instead, the players should have determined a course of action and developed necessary skills beforehand. Kristine's coaches often had pregame meetings where they would walk players through every possible situation they might encounter on the field—where to defend a corner kick, where to go for an offense free kick, and so on. By doing this, the coaches gave players the mindset to know what to do when they were on the field. They were ready for any situation, so there was no stress during the game. Mia Hamm perfectly captured the need to continuously prepare when she said, "Many people say I'm the best women's soccer player in the world. I don't think so. And because of that, some-day I just might be."[29] She knew that it would take a continuous effort to improve her skills to become the best she could be.

## Prepare as an Individual and as a Team

When it comes to preparation, teams and individuals are in a complex and dynamic relationship. Yes, there are individual efforts; however, the team must also be able to work as a unit. Each team member has specific needs that must be met by the team, and these needs need to be addressed so everyone can contribute their very best.

New team members will benefit from the experienced team members. Each team member needs to spend time practicing and hanging out with other members on the team to get to know other members of the team and what they might need from them during a game. The USWNT bonded both on and off the field, including traveling abroad, playing in front of large crowds, practicing with the team, having team meals, and serving as role models for young girls. The great amount of time they spent together allowed them to understand each other deeply; each athlete could anticipate what their team members might need during a match and prepare to meet that need.

## Onboarding

Preparation is critical for the business world too, because it is how team members gain situational awareness. Too often, we jump from talent acquisition to performance without considering the need for effectively learning how to operate as a team. In business, preparation is often limited to a brief onboarding process. For many companies, onboarding is not a priority, which significantly slows the assimilation of new team members into the company. Also, by not allowing for a formal onboarding process, the new person will take longer to acclimate and become proficient in their new role.

During onboarding, new team members should learn about the policies and standard operating procedures (SOPs) that help the team do its job

---

29  Mia Hamm, *Go for the Goal: A Champion's Guide to Winning in Soccer and Life* (New York: HarperCollins, 1999).

effectively. These SOPs define work processes and interaction points for interdependent workflows. Much like a pregame meeting, SOPs give team members the resources and information they need to do their job. The process shows them how to prioritize tasks and projects when considering all the work that must be completed. Once there, they work together to sequence and integrate tasks, track progress, and deliver on time.

Effective onboarding will show the team how to procure necessary resources, including people, finances, tools, and access to leadership. The resource planning depends upon the determined purpose, goals, and strategy. Team members should consider how they can best share resources across the team and contribute to the team's overall success.

## Practice

Practice is where roles are defined, strategy is implemented, and trust is built. We may not think of colleagues "practicing" together as they work toward a goal, but whenever a team fairly delegates work tasks as they progress through a detailed project plan and achieve deliverable milestones, they are practicing working together. During practice, the team learns these situations and what their role will be when they encounter it so they will be a unified coalition when needed.

The practice agenda should be based on what required individual tactical skills are needed (e.g., for soccer these might be ball handling, shooting, or passing), as well as what collaborative skills are needed (e.g., for business these might be compiling data, presenting research, or working together to recruit a new client). The team should be in learning mode, so mistakes are OK. Often, these team concepts are introduced and then repeated so much that they become second nature once the actual performance starts. Each practice provides situational experience that the team learns from. As practice experience builds, the day-to-day interactions increasingly provide touch points among team members.

Briana Scurry, Kristine's teammate and the first goalkeeper as well as the first black woman to be inducted into the National Soccer Hall of Fame, spoke about learning teamwork when she charged, "A champion is someone who does not settle for that day's practice, that day's competition, that day's performance. They are always striving to be better."[30]

---

30    Ann Killion, *Champions of Women's Soccer* (New York: Penguin Random House, 2018).

The USWNT's strategy to double team every player on the opposing team was an incredibly demanding strategy that required grueling training and conditioning so its athletes could be in the best shape possible. As Michelle Akers said, "We had a culture of 'extra'—doing whatever it took to be the best. I trained harder knowing that my teammates were doing the same thing and that this was what it would take to accomplish our goals."[31]

Kristine's team also practiced anticipating what their opponents might do on the field. In pregame meetings, they gained insights by looking at other teams' strategies. By doing this, they generated new ideas for their own team's strategy and improvement. Coaches detailed each player's responsibility—including the reserves. Each of these responsibilities was tied to the overall game plan, which included broader team objectives. By doing this, each player understood why their role mattered. Everyone was included. No one was insignificant.

With Coach Tony DiCicco, the team would train for different game scenarios. At practice, they would discuss and run through what to do if they were up a goal. Then they would discuss what to do if they were down a goal. Then they would practice what they would do if they were tied. Coach DiCicco would say, "OK, starting team, you are down a goal." Their objective would be to tie it up and then try to win in the time that was left. Yes, sometimes in practice they may not have succeeded. However, when they played games and were down a goal, they did not freak out because they had trained for that scenario. In other words, they were prepared.

Coach DiCicco helped his team elevate the importance and the intensity of their practice with these hypothetical drills. They built their situation awareness through detailed preparation and continuous repeat so that all were comfortable. They had intense practice battles between teammates, all to make each other better. So, when it came time to perform, the game was simply an outcome of all the training that occurred in practice. He said, "When they competed in games, they only knew maximum effort, because they duplicated match conditions every day in training."[32]

---

31   Peter Tollman, Josh Serlin, Michelle Akers, Anson Dorrance, "The Power of Inspiration, Perspiration, and Cooperation—in Sports and in Business," The Boston Consulting Group, June 13, 2018, https://www.bcg.com/publications/2018/power-inspiration-perspiration-cooperation-sports-business.aspx.

32   Tony DiCicco, Colleen Hacker, *Catch Them Being Good* (New York: Penguin Books, 2002).

## Invest in Corporate Practice

Just like sports, business teams need to set aside time to "practice" so they are confident when then need to perform. A band does not go on stage for a concert without a dress rehearsal, so why should a business team not rehearse how they are going to perform? Business teams also need time to review, rehearse, discuss, correct, and coach. The primary concept of separating practice from performance in the corporate world is providing time and opportunity for the team to develop. This is learning agility, a team capable of changing their behavior to improve performance. Then, the team will be better prepared for "game time" when their deliverable is due. Otherwise, you are throwing the team into the proverbial fire.

This all may sound pretty basic, but can you recall the last time you joined a business team and they sat down to practice these items? Most workplace teams are constantly in "perform" without the opportunity to prepare or practice. Teamwork can be learned, yet it takes time and intention. Peak performers seek excellence through a focused, confident, and consistent approach. No detail is too small when learning the fundamentals and executing them. You need purposeful and deliberate practice that simulates the real thing. This allows teams to make adjustments to their activity and process before they perform, which is the secret to an incredible performance from the start.

Here are three suggestions for how you can develop your team through practice: business simulation, team-building activities, and teamwork coaches.

## Business Simulation

Practice before performance is critical. Like an airline pilot practices in a flight simulator before flying a plane, allowing your team to practice in a controlled, low-risk condition that simulates the "perform" environment will increase their likelihood at succeeding during the real thing. The business simulations should have participants actively involved in three steps:

- Define their overall purpose and strategy.
- Collaborate—including listening, critical thinking, and resolving conflict—to execute their strategy.

- Debrief the experience to extract the key learning points that they can then "perform" in their job.

When team members engage in a business simulation and learn these critical teamwork capabilities, they also develop their leadership skills. The engaged participants experience what they will encounter at their workplace, and are better prepared to perform. This experiential learning is called "learn by doing" and is the most effective way to practice.

## Team-Building Activities

Practice can extend beyond the iteration of technical skills and include the development of relationships among team members. These "team-building activities" are popular company investments because they accelerate the trust-building process of learning about one another. For example, Kristine's team participated in an activity where each player acknowledged each other by writing down positive traits on a paper on each player's back, recognizing their strengths. These types of team-building activities put everyone on an equal playing field. By providing a different learning context, a new leader emerged using a different strength at a different time for the team to be successful.

Yet, you must know your audience when designing these activities, as the wrong match will have team members thinking the activities are a waste of time or silly. When done correctly, these team-building activities will accelerate trust among your team members.

Team leaders should always be looking for ways to better develop their team, as extracurricular activities help develop the relationships, friendships, and trust that carry over to the workplace. Take time to eat together, go to the water cooler for casual conversation, go to social activities together, or even play a competitive game of foosball (soccer in the corporate office!). Have game nights or go bowling to allow new members of the team to get to know veteran members, and for the team as a whole to have time to bond and further their camaraderie. In addition, take time to get to know what a team member likes to do outside of work during their free time. Knowing the basics about their family, their hobbies, and their interests helps you to build a rapport that is outside of your common work task.

## Teamwork Coaches

An organization has to determine if teams are going to be a part of their competitive advantage. If they decide yes, they then need to invest in teamwork. One multinational industrial conglomerate made this investment and received a significant return with teamwork effectiveness improvement. It was a huge lift by human resources (HR) yet also a key contribution to HR's credibility with the business, who saw an impact on their bottom line. This helped HR move out of the shadows to address a specific business need, improving the team interconnectivity in their structure.

To equip coaches on launching high-performing teams, this corporation trained and equipped their HR professionals to be team facilitators when a team was forming, or when it needed assistance. These HR leaders approached teamwork from a coaching perspective, teaching team members how to improve their team's performance. They wanted to see what worked instead of what didn't so they could highlight what the team members were doing well instead of focusing on what they'd done wrong.

## Perform

Coach Dorrance did not just want to win, he wanted to dominate. He inspired his team so that they, too, wanted to dominate the rankings and crush their opponents. This was especially crucial, because many view the USA as a second-class soccer nation. Kristine's team took on this feeling of national pride from Dorrance, who said, "I was going to beat them with the tools of the American spirit!"[33]

After each game, Coach Tony DiCicco facilitated a conversation to highlight the positives, asking his team to identify the things they did well in the game as a team. In addition, he asked them to identify the things they needed to work on, improve, and get better for the next game. It was not pointing fingers and placing blame; instead, it was a disciplined approach to show his team how to be more successful going forward. In addition to the tactical skill building, it

---

33  Peter Tollman, Josh Serlin, Michelle Akers, Anson Dorrance, "The Power of Inspiration, Perspiration, and Cooperation—in Sports and in Business," The Boston Consulting Group, June 13, 2018, https://www.bcg.com/publications/2018/power-inspiration-perspiration-cooperation-sports-business.aspx.

was also a team-building exercise as team members gave specific compliments to players who had done well in that game.

In addition to the immediate review after the game, they also watched game tapes to determine how they could improve for the next game. The coach provided his observations, and the team captain and team reviewed the collected data. They did this to improve teamwork from one performance to another, as well as to allow each team member an opportunity to review and revise their performance between games.

## After-Action Review

In business, you perform by driving superior results. It is often do or die. If the teamwork output is exceptional when compared to the standard, team members are happy, and the team can excel. Yet, many times teams are off to the next thing without assessing the behavior patterns that lead to success or failure. A team needs a systematic process to analyze what improvements they can make in order to make a difference. Yet, many times teams fail to assess and learn from their successes and failures.

After a major milestone in business, it is effective to have an After-Action Review similar to athletes watching films of their previous games. Originally developed by the US Army, some companies call this process "lessons learned," "post-mortems," or "hot washes." This review is a structured debrief to analyze what happened, why it happened, and how it can be done better in the future. It is meant to be a clear comparison of what your team did that was intended versus what were the actual results that the team achieved. By installing this reflection process on both team dynamics and business outcomes, you are building a culture of accountability and process improvement.

In the interview that follows, you will learn how David Heavey, Kristine's husband, is able to incorporate the principles of prepare, practice, and perform in his role as a Brookline firefighter.

## 1:1 with David Heavey

David Heavey was a two-sport athlete (golf and hockey) at the University of Connecticut. After serving as captain of the hockey team, he played semiprofessional in England before returning to the Boston area to start the fire academy, where he has served since 2001.

## How did the fire academy prepare you for working at the fire department?

Just like in hockey, every firefighter has to understand their role and what they need to do. Not everyone can score a goal. Only one person is the fastest skater, firefighter, what have you. You have to play your role to succeed. In the fire department, our work is highly complex; how we collaborate can make or break our ability to succeed in dangerous situations. As a team, our interdependence is substantial, with processes and roles designed to make us successful.

I didn't know much about firefighting when I first joined the fire department; I was at the academy for sixteen weeks. This regimented curriculum stressed teamwork, because your life depends on it. You can't do your job alone; you have to work together as a unit. Posted on our station wall today is basketball coach Phil Jackson's quote: "The strength of the team is each member. The strength of each member is the team."

When you know your place on the team, the entire system can work. If you do it well, then you can easily put a fire out. The hydrant guy attaches the hose to the hydrant; the driver knows when to open or close the engine's water line.

## How does your team practice to stay ready to respond?

When I first joined the station, I relied on the older guys to teach me, as they have been through and seen everything. When I first joined, it was a dual company so that I cross-trained on the ladder truck and engine. Today, now that I am experienced, my job is to train new hires.

Our training consists of three steps, which we continuously repeat:

1. **Discuss**—what do the trainers want to see in this drill
2. **Drill**—practice our firefighting skills (i.e., how to position the fire ladder on the building)
3. **Debrief**—Based on our drill performance, how can we execute better?

We cannot be complacent, as complacency can kill on the job. You have to be ready for an emergency. We have to practice to stay up to date.

## When you perform, what is the key to teamwork?

Lives are on the line. Whoever you are going to meet, it is their worst day, and you have to make sure everything is okay in some aspect, whether fire, car accident, or some other emergency. You have to have your "A Game" on.

When you get on the fire truck and go on the run, you are all together. It is organized chaos, and the team has to remain calm. You have to think on the go a lot as well as rely on your practice training. I have full confidence when I go on that engine that no matter what I will face, I am going to do my job and do it well. I have prepared myself physically and mentally for any task at hand.

You never know what you are going to encounter. You have to adapt quickly. You have to do something. You don't have the option to show up on a scene and do nothing. There are no "what ifs" when you are in a situation. You need that team aspect with everyone working together.

## Tactics for Your Team

Preparation, practice, and performance are integral parts of a powerhouse. Team members prepare themselves to help the team reach its potential. They then practice their teamwork process through a dress-rehearsal simulation. Finally, they perform when it's time to execute their winning strategy.

Take a moment to reflect on how you can implement these tactics in your organization. How will you:

**1.** Procure the information, training, and capabilities required to support the team?

**2.** Dedicate time for team development?

**3.** Execute business strategy so that stakeholders are satisfied with the delivery quality and/or quantity?

*Looking at this photo, Kristine said, "I love my teammates' celebrations. This is Michelle Akers, arguably the best player to ever play the game, Shannon Macmillan, and me celebrating Michelle's penalty kick in the 1999 World Cup semifinals against Brazil." They went on to win 2–0 at Stanford Stadium. (Credit: J. Brett Whitesell/isiphotos.com)*

# Communicating within the Team

*"When we stepped on the field for a game, we relied on that interconnectedness. We were at our best."*

**—Michelle Akers**

Communication is vital in all aspects of life. On the soccer field it is just another part of success. Kristine remembers during her career when games weren't going so well, one of the key reasons was communication; players weren't talking on the field. It wasn't necessarily that the players weren't telling each other what to do or how to do it; instead they were missing the words of support and encouragement that built togetherness and team. One of the loneliest times on the field is when you don't know if you have support behind you or next to you. However, when you hear, "Keep them outside" or "I'm here, win it," you don't feel as isolated or alone. Words of encouragement fire you up throughout a game. Nonverbal communication too, such as the high fives or thumbs up that let your teammate know they are okay.

An assist, which is passing the ball to another player so that person can score a goal, is the ultimate representation of teamwork. When a player chooses to pass the ball to a teammate who has a better opportunity on goal, it is not only unselfish but smart. Anson Dorrance, University of North Carolina Women's Soccer Coach, always told his players, "If you are in the attacking third of the field, do not pass the ball unless the person you are passing to will score a goal." You have to know as a player where your teammates are and what is the best choice to make in that moment. Being aware of all these aspects as you are getting closer to your goal is vital to the success of your team. Abby Wambach agrees; she shares, "I've never scored a goal in my life without getting a pass from someone else."

Over the course of her career, Kristine had 103 career assists, second only to Mia Hamm. Kristine is proud of her contributions to her team's success. For Kristine, having an assist was just as important as scoring.

## Why Communicating Is Important

In the business world, high-performing teams are required to work in new, agile ways. Fast-moving, cross-functional teams rely on efficient communication and effective collaboration, not simple, cordial conversation. This communication builds inclusive teams who can explain ideas and opinions, share critical information, solicit feedback, and resolve conflicts. These teams know their common objectives, goals, and strategy. They know that if the team is successful, they will accomplish more than the sum of their individual achievements.

Leaders are in charge of ensuring that messages are delivered consistently to their stakeholders. Information needs to be shared as soon as it is available. Timely delivery is important because even a good message needs the recipient ready to receive it. The dialogue should be consistent, constant, and complete. In addition, you should choose the appropriate method or channel to deliver the message. Your team won't complain about you overcommunicating. If work tasks require greater interactivity, the communication should increase.

For example, imagine a scenario where an enterprise software sales team called on Fortune 500 accounts to understand what solution each company was looking for over the next three years. The team would need a core account manager to serve as the point of contact with the prospect and to "quarterback" the sales strategy. This role would identify who they need to get buy-off from to get a "yes" from the decision makers. They could then assign sales specialists to each of these stakeholders and work the account together. At weekly calls, they could determine the prospect's pain points and how the company could measure success so that all members of the sales team can align and position their solution with one overall campaign message. They could provide case studies that prove their proposed point of success. Essentially, they collaborate effectively to accomplish their team goal.

Unfortunately, this kind of collaborative, working in tandem, is not common. Many sales departments are more like the Tower of Babel, where people don't speak the same language, if they speak at all. With undercommunicating, there is confusion among the team that leads to guesses, gossip, and disconnects. This often creates tension. Instead, a powerhouse communicates effectively by following three principles: listen, network, and collaborate.

# Become an Effective Listener

Listening is one of the most critical components of collaboration and communication. A new person coming into a team without first listening is not well received. On a high-caliber team like Kristine's, you had to be able to listen. Kristine's team had a pecking order, where rookies took it all in without saying much as they got grounded and built confidence. Of course, there was always a place where young players could have their voices heard by a captain or the coach, but most new players appreciated the time to learn. And sometimes it is by listening that our words gain weight.

When the USWNT was playing Norway in the World Cup in 2003, the game was also a qualifier for the Olympics. At halftime, one of the team's informal leaders was all fired up. She was vocal, intense, and encouraging to her team. It wasn't what she said that affected her teammates—it was her emotion, passion, and tone. Because she didn't speak often, the team tuned in more whenever she talked. When she spoke, her teammates listened.

## Power of Listening

It's amazing how common it is for people to forget the power of listening as they become more powerful themselves. One tech executive enlisted a high-priced coach, and after a year of coaching said that he had learned "to be a better listener." Another CEO was surprised to hear that his rambling was hurting the effectiveness of the team discussion. Most people aren't aware of how to practice effective listening and successful communication techniques to achieve team goals. Listening is one of the greatest strengths of a team, and the failure to listen can be a team's biggest failure.

## Pay Attention

To become a better listener and thus a more collaborative team member, you must pay attention. Many times others will know that you have "tuned out," so try to not let your mind wander. You want your team to know that you will listen to what they say, otherwise they will not give you all the information you may need to make a decision. One CEO keeps a sign on her desk that says, "Be Present." When employees come to talk with her, this sign is the first indication that she will pay attention and listen. In addition, it sets the criteria that she expects full attention from them in return.

Teams should seek input from each team member, as each has something unique to contribute. For example, Walt Disney was legendary for discussing ideas with everyone in order to improve their company's product and service. He asked questions of everyone, regardless of the person's position, down to the tactical details of asking the janitors where the best location for trash cans should be in order to minimize litter at the theme park. His employees knew things that he did not, and he never took that for granted. Yet, many leaders do not take the time to ask front-line employees questions and then listen to their answers for insights. Consequently, many employees don't feel heard.

To help ensure that your employees know you're paying attention, make eye contact, or as a youth soccer coach says, "Listen with your eyes."

## Keep an Open Mind

A good listener suspends judgment so that a discussion is not one-sided, or simply "reflective listening." You need an open mind to avoid shutting down another person's contribution. When you do not keep your mind open, then your "conversation" is actually a pair of monologues in the presence of another person.

You should be able to discuss your team members' ideas without providing your opinions until they have all contributed. This will create a sense of belonging since each team member knows the other's perspective, and it helps you have the input you need for decision making. What would be the point of hiring a good team member with excellent experience and potential if you're not going to trust them? If you've selected the right team members, you should never have a one-sided conversation with them, as they bring value to the table that will not be heard during a monologue.

Team members process information differently. While some think out loud, others will take longer to process information silently. If dealing with the latter, you need to give them the time they need to fully process the information. This is especially true when working with people who speak foreign languages. You must allow time for them to translate in their heads and prepare their responses. However, many Western-based workers are not comfortable with these pauses of silence. In fact, the Western culture is almost starting your sentence before the previous speaker is done; whereas, in other cultures, a pause between native speakers is more common. As the leader, you'll need to reassure both types of people that they will have the space they need to fully form their insights before sharing them.

## Understand Others

When you fully invest in understanding what the other person's perspective is, they'll know. As popular author Stephen Covey said, "Seek first to understand, then to be understood." It is not what is said, it is what is heard. Many of us have a tendency to provide immediate solutions to what someone is telling us about instead of drawing out critical information and trying to understand how and why someone is seeking your advice. Instead, summarize what you heard by repeating back in your own words what you think the other person has asked to ensure you genuinely understand what is being shared—the speaker's beliefs, expectations, and requests.

A business school dean has a rule of thumb to listen 80 percent of the time and only speak 20 percent. He also says that 20 percent should be full of questions instead of having one's own say. He uses inquiry to fully understand what is going on, seeking to understand and challenge the assumptions below the conversation's surface. The dean then ends the conversation by asking, "Is there anything left that you have not told me? Is anything that we have discussed unclear? Is there any other information you need that I have not yet provided?" These questions effectively communicate his desire to help the person he is speaking to, as well as offer the opportunity for any necessary clarification. Most appreciate these kind of opportunities to be heard and understood.

## Respond

Once others have had an opportunity to share, you should respond respectfully. When you speak, pay attention to how you begin the dialogue; the first few words will set the context for whatever comes next. You can use simple acknowledgments such as, "Thanks for sharing" or "uh huh." When a team member presents an idea, for example, if you start your response with "no," you'll create a defensive environment. This creates two options for the team member, neither of which are good: fight or flight. There is also the "Yes, but" response, which is a dirty yes. It does not feel sincere and is somewhat confusing.

A simple "Yes, and" is agreeable and reinforcing, and it sets the foundation for moving on to improve the concept with another idea. Essentially, it is team members bringing bricks to build a collaborative solution together. This transparency improves the team's understanding of one another.

So for maximum impact, effective communication is a two-way street, with genuine solicitation of feedback and mutual respect between parties. If you are wanting to be a good listener, do not interrupt others, and definitely avoid formulating a response while the other person is talking.

# Understand Social Networks

Communication always takes place within a social network. An employee develops relationships with many different people in their organization, forming these social networks. These networks can be functional, helping the members of the network demonstrate higher performance and commitment. Or, they can be dysfunctional—impeding, ostracizing, and sabotaging the work of others.

## Team Member Relationships

There are primarily two types of social relationships within a workplace network. First is an employee's relationship with his or her leader. Second is an employee's relationship with his team members. Both of these relationship types influence the employee's attitudes, behavior, performance, and engagement. Although these relationships are different, they occur simultaneously and impact each other.

You can begin to understand the nuances of your social network by performing a social network analysis.[34] This inventory diagnoses the sum of the team's interactions by indicating where a team member goes to when they need information, desire another perspective, seek coaching, or want to solve a problem. Through this social network analysis, we can better understand how teams collaborate to solve their business challenges. If we understand the structure of the network, we can also identify potential blind spots and obstacles to team performance.

So, when analyzing one's social network of organizational relationships, strong network relationships are characterized by mutual trust, advice giving and seeking, mentoring, and accountability, and they answer the question of "How do we work together?" In addition, a network of strong team member relationships may compensate for a low-quality leader/coach relationship.

Weak network relationships are characterized by distance, skepticism, and limited interaction, and answer the question of "What can I gain from you?" This develops a sense of self-interest, separation, apathy, and discouragement toward their work that the leader cannot eliminate. A weak team member relationship can actually be detrimental to performance, because there is no pressure to perform.

## Network Centrality

In addition to the strength or weakness of a team member relationship, a social network also identifies the team member's degree of centrality to the network. Centrality is the degree of connectedness an individual has in the network. If someone is high in network centrality, then there is a greater amount of information flow, contributing to a higher degree of control and influence. Due to the access to information, knowledge, and advice, a central team member knows who to go to for task-related advice, performance feedback, and emotional support. Basically, they are more effective at mining the network's strengths to optimize team performance. Thus, an employee with high centrality is likely to have high performance, engagement, and commitment to the team.

---

34  Lynette Gillis, "A Network Perspective of Multiple Social Exchange Relationships," University of Texas Libraries (2008), https://repositories.lib.utexas.edu/ handle/2152/3852.

In a study of Dutch soccer players, researchers witnessed intense collaboration and synergy among the players. The friendships between team members impacted their performance on the soccer field. The stronger the person's relationships, the more central that team member was in the team social network. The more central the team member to the network, then the higher the impact was on performance.

In addition, if a team member has an accurate perception of another team member's capabilities, that, too, positively impacted work performance. For example, you know which team member is a better passer and which one is a better shooter. This benefits cross-understanding of collaboration. All of this impacted the Dutch players' performance and development, as the relationships provide advice, feedback, and emotional support. So, the Dutch soccer leader knows to cultivate player relationships to improve performance for their soccer club.[35]

The structure of the network and the quality of network relationships is important to organizational outcomes. These networks affect career development, power, conflict resolution, and creativity. Strong team member relationships improve performance through information sharing, advice giving, and social pressure, as well as employee engagement.

By knowing the importance of the network, a team should intentionally build a strong social network among team members and nourish these relationships, ensuring that all members are highly connected. To build these effective social networks, leaders should invest in mentoring relationships, organizational and team social events, training, and team-building activities.

## Collaborate

The final characteristic of strong team communication is collaboration. A team needs transparent and open communication to effectively exchange information among team members. For a team to effectively share knowledge, they must learn how to communicate effectively on interdisciplinary teams. Through transparent communication, the team members combine

---

35  Jing Han and Kevin Van Dongen, "Friendship Network Centrality and the Performance of Soccer Players: The Role of Cognitive Accuracy," *Human Performance* 28, no. 3 (2015): 265–279.

their knowledge and experiences, commit to a shared goal, align interdependent work, and make decisions to get around roadblocks.[36]

Yet, sometimes what a team says and what a team does is different, as there is not transparent communication. There is the foreground conversation, which is what is said during the meeting, and then there is the background conversation that they save for gossip at the water cooler. This background conversation happens because individuals know that the collective decision discussed at the meeting is not the best decision for the team. In this situation, team members become pessimistic, resentful, confused, skeptical, and negative.

When Kristine played at UNC, one senior was a third-string goalie who never played but had always practiced hard for four years. This player was a positive force on the team, working hard for continuous improvement even while knowing that she might never play. Coach Dorrance decided to sub her in as a field player during the national championship final. UNC had a big lead against their opponent, and Kristine, understanding this player's contribution and collaboration over the past four years, took it upon herself to give her a game experience that she would always remember. Kristine took the ball down the left side before delivering it on a platter to this player, who was waiting in the box. This player ripped the shot into the back corner of the net! A dogpile ensued as the entire team celebrated with her. The joyous moment created an unbelievable memory for this player. Kristine had collaborated with this teammate to make sure she scored in the national championship.

Team members are always interdependent on other team members. On the soccer field, players must play to "spaces," knowing and trusting that their team member will anticipate the move and also step to the right space at the right time. Off the soccer field, a team with stars must also moderate their individuality without overshadowing other team members so that the team shines. Yes, many teams have stars; yet, this can be detrimental if the team does not come first. Otherwise, it can create a divisive environment, creating competing factions within a team.

When Michelle Akers was hurt and not able to play in the game, Captain Carla Overbeck wrote on her ankle tape "Mufasa," Michelle's nickname that

---

36  Francois Chiocchio, Daniel Forgues, David Paradis, and Ivanka Iordanova, "Teamwork in Integrated Design Projects: Understanding the Effects of Trust, Conflict, and Collaboration on Performance," *Project Management Journal* 42, no. 6 (2011): 78–91.

celebrates her big hair. While Michelle wasn't there on the field, the team was playing for her, and Carla's simple, small act showed that Michelle was still part of the team. The team's cohesiveness showed in their care for each other.

## Synchronize

Working together is all about collaboration, not cooperation. To cooperate means that individuals work separately and independently on previously defined tasks. Collaborative behavior is a synchronous activity designed to solve a common problem together. Collaboration is often talked about yet usually vague in concrete rules, and even more challenging to measure when you try to delineate responsibility/accountability. Collaboration is critical for effective teamwork, almost to the point that it is a synonym for the concept.

A team must be coordinated so that each individual's contributions are synchronized. This heightened synchronicity helps with task coordination. The team operates in a harmonized fashion when cognitive, verbal, or behavioral activities are effectively expressed. These collective actions and inputs convert to productive outcomes. For example, in a successful manufacturing environment, the engineer needs to be coordinated with fabrication, who is synchronized with production, who in turn has harmonized efforts with sales. Without this coordination among team members and departments, the team will fall out of synch, and performance and production will suffer.

## Prioritize

Each team member's contributions to the overall deliverable should be balanced, with respect to each member's specific knowledge and experience. At this point, it is important to distinguish between taskwork and teamwork. Taskwork is how an individual team member interacts with tasks, tools, machines, and systems using their own knowledge, skills, and abilities. Teamwork, on the other hand, is how team members combine their thoughts, actions, and feelings to coordinate, adapt, and reach their common goals. The effort for each team member should specify what taskwork must be shared so that individuals know when they should reach out to their colleagues for support and resources.

Collaboration depends on prioritizing the team's tasks over other obligations. This development and growth indicate the team's capacity to manage itself. As the team develops, its perceptions of goal interdependence will affect how the team members acquire, share, and use knowledge to make effective decisions. When each team member is playing for each other, they have to prioritize. As an equity partner in an accounting firm once remarked, "Collaboration is not rocket science. It is harder."

## Support

A team needs mutual support, where team members display respect by developing other team members' ideas and contributions rather than trying to compete with each other. Fostering this mutual support helps build trust and manage conflict. A team member's perception of the team's level of support will affect their performance. This person's perception is shaped by their attitudes, values, cognitions, and motivations. These supportive moments can be a literal high five on the soccer field, a "good job" comment during the business team meeting, or some other kind of shout-out to a team member.

One of the best examples of support is a team of doctors treating a patient with a complex diagnosis. Each doctor does not have all the training and expertise to address each ailment, so a cohesive team of doctors is needed to effectively treat the patient. It goes beyond simple file sharing of medical records. This type of team requires trust and respect, as each doctor provides specific analysis of the patient in their area of expertise in order to derive the best overall treatment plan for their patient.

Communication is the glue that holds a powerhouse together. It is the lifeblood of these teams. Michelle Akers, one of the greatest if not the greatest soccer player in women's history, was the cornerstone of her team. In the 1:1 section that follows, you will learn more about how these three principles support the teamwork strategy of communicating during Michelle's career: active listening, the social network, and collaboration.

## 1:1 with Michelle Akers

Michelle Akers was a legend during the 1991 and 1999 Women's World Cup victories. She was named FIFA Female Player of the Century in 2002 along with China's Sun Wen, as well as being awarded the FIFA Order of Merit in 1998, their highest honor for her contributions to the game of soccer. She was inducted into soccer's National Hall of Fame in 2004. Before this, she won the Hermann Trophy as the top collegiate player in 1988.

## How did active listening have a positive impact on teamwork when you were playing for Coach DiCicco?

I had some tiredness issues and was trying to figure out what to do about it. I was eventually diagnosed with chronic fatigue syndrome. Little was known about it at the time. My doctor at Johns Hopkins in Baltimore talked with the team physician and Coach Tony DiCicco.

Learning how to succeed despite this illness came from my relationship with Coach DiCicco. He listened and learned about the disease. We talked about what the team could do differently to accommodate my illness going forward, including what was going to work and what wasn't. There weren't definite answers, so we had to experiment. I always wanted to do my job and contribute. I didn't want to take someone else's place. He bet the farm on me. He communicated with the team about why I was "half-dead" sometimes. Tony prolonged my career, changing my position to enable me to play. He trusted my judgment and allowed me to set my own pace. He had faith in me to not let the team down. Hardly anyone does that. He was very special and enlightened.

## How did the social network impact the team?

I had thirty surgeries during my career, so everyone knew my routine: surgery, rehab, back on the field. I would go through anything to give to the team. In 1995, I was playing China and got knocked out on a corner kick during the first ten minutes of the game. I was hoping to come back, yet didn't get back until the semis and was still not 100 percent. If the team is focused on just me, then the game is lost. That is your downfall, relying on one player too much.

In 1999, I was playing a defensive corner at the end of the game. I went for the ball and was punched in the head. I said I could keep playing, yet someone dragged me off the field. There was a small TV in the training room so I could see the winning penalty kick. When we won, they were not going to keep me from the podium. As I walked to it, the crowd was chanting my name, which is such a powerful thing and so very special! In the locker room afterward, I wanted champagne with the rest of the team but had to settle for IVs in my arm.

Now I hear "she was a 99er." When I ask, "What do you mean?" the answer is that the team in 1999 was different than any other team. It had grit, resolve, mentality, and they still have it even off the field. I get that comment because I can feel it, yet I can't explain it. Everyone loved to play, and we loved the people we were playing with. The harder the game, the better it was, as it was so much fun to be a part of! It was a commitment to that vision, and this fed into the energy that was unstoppable.

## How does a team best collaborate?

We had lost to Norway in the World Cup in 1995 and were preparing for the 1996 Olympics. I loved playing against them because they were so tough and brought out our best, but I'll never forget that loss. At practice, we were standing on the line and running fitness, basically getting our guts run off. I always ran next to Kristine; she was quicker than me on the turns. She would always say, "C'mon Mich!" to be motivating and inspiring. She pulled you along to be better, even though she was being challenged during the run also.

On another instance, it was cold and raining in San Diego at the Olympic training center. After the practice, Kristine was upset and said, "It is just so easy to try." That is the key to success, just trying. It is easy to try, yet this is not apparent. It is just the try, the working hard for ninety minutes during the game. This passes on into your life long after your soccer days are done. So many people don't try because they didn't prepare and are afraid to fail.

People would tell us on the USWNT that "you guys never lose." We did. Every day in practice. Our practices tended to be harder than our games. We depended on our teammates to kick our butt on a daily basis. Commitment and mentality: If they were lowered, this affected the team. If someone was not giving their all, then it impacted the team. We benefited from the tough practice, as this gave us our edge when we were playing Brazil or Norway. When we stepped on the field for a game, we relied on that interconnectedness. We were at our best. When I walked out there, I knew we could crush anybody.

## Tactics for Your Team

Communicating effectively within the team includes active listening so that team members can be present and seek to understand others. It also entails establishing a social network so that team members understand whom the central person is and are able to communicate effectively with them. And last, it entails collaboration so that each member of the team is able to work together as a unit, rather than independently.

Consider the following. How will you:

1. Be present and actively listen to team members when they are sharing?

2. Locate the center of the social network whom team members access for work performance?

3. Interact effectively with team members to achieve desired outcomes?

*"My favorite thing about playing soccer was my teammates. This photo shows Julie Foudy and I celebrating after a goal I scored against Australia in the 2004 Olympics in Greece," Kristine said. "Scoring feels so much better when you have teammates to share it with." (Credit: Michael Pimentel/isiphotos.com)*

# Handling Team Conflict

*"Athletics brings out a side of you that is wonderful.*
*It brings out so many good attributes like*
*competing, intensity, and playing at the highest level."*

**—Julie Foudy**

When working with a group of competitive, strong-minded people who are full of personalities, conflict is bound to surface. Everything on the USWNT was not always roses. Tension sometimes came between team members. For the most part, these conflicts stayed in the locker room, and after the tensions eased, things would be back to normal.

One particular situation happened a lot at trainings. One player had a tendency to always step on feet during practice. It wasn't on purpose, but it hurt, and the players still had to play. Tensions were high. Sometimes a foul would be called, and the player would apologize. This is how they dealt with it in an effective manner, and the team would always joke about it later. They never let tension stand in the way of purpose.

# Why Addressing Conflict Is Important

Similar to Kristine's experience on the soccer field, in the business world there are always others who encroach on your job and "step on your toes." All teams, be they in sports or business, have conflict. The key with conflict is not that it exists, but rather how a team dissipates the conflict in order to bring everyone together again. No one wants to be on a painful team walking on eggshells. This conflict will tear the team apart. Out of all key tactics in this book, the mismanagement of conflict is the biggest potential derailer for any team. A powerhouse must respond effectively, disagree constructively, and mediate conflict.

## Respond Effectively

To be an effective team, you must not try to blindly eradicate conflict, as there will always be disagreements. Instead, you must learn how to address conflict effectively by addressing it in a way that will strengthen the team. In the instance with the conflict on Kristine's team, they did not let the negative energy become contagious or destructive.

Conflicts are obstacles that can bring a team together and strengthen the team. Or, they can cause a team to fall apart. Some have said that overcoming barriers to performance is how a group becomes a team. Players on the bench want to be on the field, and if they see a player on the field not doing as well as they should, that can create negative energy and conflict rooted in a player trying to take another's place. It is the same thing in the business world when a manager may not lead a team effectively and another colleague may attempt to stake their territory or gain favor in the eyes of their C-Suite. Instead of destroying each other, teams need to be supportive.

## Handle Pressure

Conflict always surfaces, especially when a team has to perform complex tasks under pressure.

Kristine had pressure to perform on the field with everyone watching, not unlike company leaders who perform with the market analyzing their decisions. Tasks like meeting quarterly earnings goals, project milestones, and reallocating budgets are common activities that create extreme pressure and tension. Executive-level people are not the only ones who deal with pressure;

team members at any level can experience conflict, due to real or perceived differences. This affects teamwork, resulting in lower effectiveness, reduced well-being, and employee turnover. Research shows that the degree of conflict present on any team is typically affected by the complexity of the task, the amount of pressure and how well the team can handle the pressure, the size of the team dealing with it, the experience they bring to the situation, and the degree to which individual team members need one another to perform their tasks.[37] However, a team cannot allow this pressure to jeopardize its results.

For example, during a large merger and acquisition (M&A), two companies needed to assimilate into one new organization. One company's CEO became COO of the new company with the promise that he would eventually become CEO. The other company's CEO remained active in executive decision making even after the merger, despite the newly coined COO's promised promotion. In the boardroom, this caused issues, as the team essentially had two leaders voicing their opinion—the current CEO and the future CEO. When a decision had to be made weighing short-term impact versus long-term consequences, they obviously had two different perspectives, with competing motivations based on who would be in charge of the company when the plans would be set in motion. The two CEOs and their teams had to learn how to prioritize the mission of the organization, accelerate trust, determine the operating principles for the newly formed executive team, and align to the same language for the merged company. With both a current and future CEO operating under intense pressure for the merger to be successful when so many acquisitions fail, the C-Suite conflict threatened the outcome.

## Task Conflict

A task conflict is a "what to do disagreement" or issue that arises from the process of working toward a goal. These sorts of conflicts tend to motivate team members to find the optimal decision. When there are task conflicts, team members disagree about specific actions required to complete the project. Solving these problems requires rich bidirectional communication between team members

---

37   Carsten K.W. De Dreu and Annelies E.M. Van Vianen, "Managing relationship conflict and the effectiveness of organizational teams," *Journal of Organizational Behavior* 22, no. 3 (May 2001): 309–328, https://onlinelibrary.wiley.com/doi/abs/10.1002/job.71.

who are driven by a willingness to collaborate. Ideally, rather than a compromise or concession by one team member, a team can have a civil negotiation to find a constructive solution. This exchange leads to a deeper understanding of the overall task issues and the optimal plan for the successful attainment of goals.

For example, one company in the petroleum industry focused on the upstream part of the supply chain, finding and producing the crude oil and natural gas. This exploration sector did well, and the company was a top producer. The company wanted to expand into the downstream part of the supply chain that included oil refinery and distribution, which upstream leaders perceived to be an action against their established strengths. Thus, this goal took a lot of task action and completion to reach fruition, as the downstream leader encouraged his team to "keep building bridges" with the upstream team to influence the original organization's leaders. They were successful because the team relied on these bridges for slow growth, not pushing a big bang approach that would have alienated many relationships. There was a lot of history with the company, and they knew to take time to achieve success. Through a savvy approach of multiple tasks, the downstream leader effectively managed the healthy conflict with the upstream leaders.

## Relationship Conflict

Different than task conflict, there is also relationship conflict. When a team has a relationship conflict, team effectiveness and satisfaction suffer. It is personal. Relationship conflicts consist of disagreements based on interpersonal issues, political norms and values, and personal taste. These conflicts arise from differences in power, personalities, and experiences. Because our personal identities are deep rooted and acquired throughout our life, the tensions created by relationship conflict are difficult to address. All teams have an interpersonal context, where perceived incompatibilities, discrepancies, irreconcilable desires, or discrepant views evolve into behavioral reactions.

Relationship conflict often originates in task conflict. For example, a communications microteam with a tight deadline for a global technology implementation was led by an antagonistic leader who was incompatible with the other microteams. Their task conflict, such as ignoring advice on how to communicate locally in a specific country, eventually led to relationship conflict when she publicly berated other team leaders on the implementation team.

The communication team was supposed to be central in distributing project knowledge, yet the relationship conflict that she created resulted in people avoiding her. Thus, the project communications were incomplete, her micro-team performed well below expectations, and the overall project suffered.

Relationship conflict is difficult because there often does not tend to be a middle ground or a mutually acceptable solution. Usually, a give and take does not solve these disagreements, and neither team member is satisfied with the outcome. Instead, the conflict becomes intractable and creates a dark cloud that looms over the team.

The insights uncovered in a relationship conflict can also be unrelated to the task that the team is working on as they relate more to the issues individual team members bring to the situation than the situation itself. These negative emotions appear, and there are negative consequences for a team member's well-being, personal identity, feelings of self-worth, and thus work effectiveness.

For example, one company had significant tension between the chief legal officer and the chief operating officer. Both were highly qualified for their roles and performed their tasks well. Yet, the tension between the two affected the rest of the executive team. The CEO stepped in to mitigate the relationship conflict, with the assistance of the chief human resources officer, for the betterment of the executive team and by extension, the organization. It was not an overnight turnaround, yet through intentional and ongoing coaching, the CEO was able to repair the relationship conflict on his executive team.

## Acknowledge Conflict

Team interactions affect the attitudes of all team members. Acknowledging that your team will have conflict sooner or later prepares you to know how to effectively manage it when it does happen so that you can bring things to a healthy resolution. How a team handles conflict is one of the critical components for how you define a team culture. A team should be able to openly say what it really thinks in a civil and constructive manner, bifurcating the challenges and solutions from the individual personas in the group. This is especially so when members engage in healthy debate with spirited and candid dialogue. These challenges help a team discover multiple perspectives on an issue in order to find an optimal solution to solve the problem. Research has shown that conflict has been associated with greater innovation and more effective interpersonal relations.[38] This is often the reason that diversity among team members is encouraged, in order to approach decisions with different perspectives.

## Disagree Constructively

USWNT Coach Tony DiCicco summarized how a team handles conflict when he remarked, "To some, challenges are exhausting. To others, they are opportunities in waiting."[39] Handling team conflict involves teaching team members how to constructively disagree with each other, and managing any such conflicts. A soccer team has different systems to position players on the field, determining how many players are on offense versus midfield versus defense. When Kristine's coach would talk through different systems with the team, he would ask for their feedback. There were often differences of opinion as they discussed each option. Yet, in the end, after a healthy discussion where everyone voiced their opinions, there would be buy-in to the final decision. Usually, a majority of people were on the same page. The challenge is if the minority spreads negative feelings, as this can spread like a disease on your team. If this is the case, it becomes much harder to deal with the conflict.

### Disagree and Commit

You know you have reached the next level of teamwork when one team member understands another team member's opposing point of view because they speak their mind—without creating a tense team environment or getting personal. They have invested in one another enough to value each other's perspective. Even in tough times, the team keeps going to overcome the challenges. This is constructive disagreement—staying friends and staying committed while disagreeing. In business, consensus is not always possible and

---

38  Carsten K.W. De Dreu and Annelies E.M. Van Vianen, "Managing relationship conflict and the effectiveness of organizational teams," *Journal of Organizational Behavior* 22, no. 3 (May 2001): 309–328, https://onlinelibrary.wiley.com/doi/abs/10.1002/job.71.

39  Tony DiCicco, Colleen Hacker, *Catch Them Being Good* (New York: Penguin Books, 2002).

actually rare, so it is critical that team members can disagree and then commit to the leader's decision.

## Address the Issue

Teams need to develop a positive team climate. To prevent relationship conflict, a team should establish, build, nurture, and maintain team trust. This trust, based on interpersonal liking and shared norms and values, leads to a high level of consensus without group think. A team member will know that others have their back. This culture not only enhances the work environment, it reduces relationship conflict levels. A mature team can diffuse tension quickly. Some call this direct and powerful discussion "candor with care," as the leader says what they mean without mixing messages with ambiguous word choice. A team must focus on addressing the problem, or the elephant in the room, while not hurting each other.

As you address the elephant, remember that the desired outcome is not consensus, but an agreement about how to move forward. Leaders will focus on the tasks to be completed, even if the elephant is a huge relationship conflict. The leader needs to establish explicit behavioral expectations on how team members should interact when discussing the problem so that the discussion remains productive—and hold team members accountable to these standards as they respond to the problem.

## Mediate Conflict

It is impossible to prevent conflict; a team needs to know how to respond when it does happen, as that response will affect the team's functioning and effectiveness.

In 1995, the USWNT fought for the "rights to our feet." This stand was to have the opportunity to seek individual endorsements for the shoes that they would wear in a game. At the time, one athletic company sponsored the USWNT team from head to toe, including their shoes. This meant players were unable to seek and benefit from additional sponsorship. Then, Michelle Akers had an opportunity to receive an endorsement from another athletic company, which caused a conflict. Other team members also wanted to be able to seek sponsorship, so they needed to respond effectively and united in order to solve the conflict and receive the desired individual sponsorship. This question was the start of the women's national team recognizing they had rights. They raised this conflict of interest, pursued and negotiated for their individual rights, and won the right to their feet.

Kristine's team captains took care of business. They put out proverbial fires when most of the team or the public didn't even know there was a fire. However, when a full team discussion did need to happen, the team captains facilitated a conversation so they could hear everyone's opinion. The strength of their leadership was that they never avoided anything. They dealt with the issues head-on, whether that was talking with the head coach about the team being burned out or talking with unhappy players so they could understand each player's perspective. USWNT Coach Tony DiCicco would counsel the players saying, "Don't whine. Find the positive in difficult situations."[40]

As team captain, Kristine was a voice for the team as well as a voice within the team. The captain's role is critical when the team needs to overcome their dysfunctions, such as disappointments or resentments about playing time. Players needed to see the overall team goals instead of just tracking their own playing time. To help mitigate these conflicts, Kristine had to be in tune with each player's personal challenges, especially when each player was separated from their support system during away games.

Like Michelle Akers and the team captains, how you mediate conflict is a conscious choice. There are three types of responses: assertive, aggressive, and avoiding.[41]

## Assertive Response

An assertive response moves toward a collaborative mindset. In this instance, the person is more likely to actively solve the issue by working out a mutually acceptable solution. Team members will elicit trustworthy information, as well as acknowledge others' feelings and opinions about the situation. If you'd like to encourage your team to respond assertively, begin the discussion

40    Tony DiCicco, Colleen Hacker, *Catch Them Being Good* (New York: Penguin Books, 2002).

41    Carsten K.W. De Dreu and Annelies E.M. Van Vianen, "Managing relationship conflict and the effectiveness of organizational teams," *Journal of Organizational Behavior* 22, no. 3 (May 2001): 309–328, https://onlinelibrary.wiley.com/doi/abs/10.1002/job.71.

by fleshing out the topic in order to generate knowledge together to ultimately reach a mutually agreed-upon decision.

## Aggressive Response

An aggressive response is when someone moves against the conflict with a contending mindset, either overtly or silently. This type of response is more likely to escalate the situation, because one team member is trying to impose their will, want, or perspective upon another. As a result, the room gets more heated and the team's trust is completely undermined. This results in poor outcomes, as team members are attacking or defending, usually leading to rejecting the team member or retreating from the team.

If you find yourself against an aggressive responder, it is critical to deescalate the situation immediately. Remember, the goal is to ascertain the feasibility of solutions, not to spiral down with anger and frustration. This may call for a "time out" by simply asking for a follow-up meeting later, in order to allow both sides to breathe and regain their composure. However, most respond with an equally aggressive response. You will not create a solution with an aggressive response; you will only create regrets.

## Avoiding Response

An avoiding response is exactly what it sounds like, as it buries or ignores the problem so that people do not have to have a difficult conversation, leaving things unsaid. Many team members choose the option of "let's not go there" to avoid "rocking the boat." Instead, leaders need to be comfortable making waves, yet usually the metaphors such as "hide in a cave" or "go to the balcony" indicate a detached, distracted approach during a conflict. This may result in shorter team meetings, yet it also means that the tough discussions that the team needs to have are not happening. Conformity breeds calm and quiet, yet that is really just the calm before the brewing storm. The good news is this does not escalate conflict, and the tension and frustration may reduce so that it no longer hurts the task work. However, avoiding does not solve conflict.

Typically, in this environment, a team member may nominally acknowledge another team member's previous statement, saying "right," "but," or "also." Yet, they do not try to settle or engage the preceding comment and instead make a different point. This may, in turn, cause multiple topics to be raised at the same time with responses overlapping one another. In this circular discussion, team members are not engaging head-on with a direct argument. This is not ideal, because it does not produce a solution.

## Drive toward Decision

With an assertive approach, you need to drive discussion toward a decision. Diffuse the tension, reduce the friction, manage the disagreement, and remove the obstacle that is causing the conflict. Make sure that you and others on your team understand the cause and effect of the issue, as well as the implications of the proposed solution, before making a decision.

For example, a consultant once received his annual performance review, which indicated that his client approach was unsatisfactory because he transparently told the client that the consulting company did not have a specific tool that was promised in the contract. The consultant's perspective was that he had been honest with the client, even though he felt that the consulting company wanted him to be unethical and mislead the client about this tool. If he had taken an avoidance approach, then his manager would not have known about his thoughts on the company's unethical practice. If he had taken an aggressive approach, then he would have created a downward spiral of conflict with his manager. Instead, the consultant took an assertive approach and calmly explained to his manager the proactive steps he took to develop an agreeable tool solution with their client.

For task conflict, a team leader needs to make roles and responsibilities clear, set the team's standards and expectations, and establish the team's deadlines and desired outcomes/results. Instead of just talking, a leader needs to hold team members' feet to the fire when they don't adhere to the team's agreed-upon rules of engagement. When you do so with transparency, you are resolving by thinking through the issue, providing feedback, and collectively coming up with a solution. It's important to take the high road, as your ultimate goal is to find a solution that is best for the team so that the conflict does not become a roadblock. As a leader, even when things get bad, you do not shift blame or desert your team members. Instead, you protect.

## Self-Regulate

A team leader also has a role in constructive disagreement and conflict response. How you handle the conflict can make or break your career, so choose your response approach wisely. It is easy to get your noise out of joint, yet as the leader you need to demonstrate self-regulation, to proactively manage your emotions and impulses. For constructive disagreement, the team leader should take a risk and make herself vulnerable before everyone else, in order to encourage debate. This means the leader does not have to project a perfect image, and instead she should authentically represent her true self.

Most critically, when the dysfunctions do lead to a conflict response, the team leader sets the tone for the entire team, whether their response is assertive, aggressive, or avoiding. It is beneficial to the team if the leader assertively approaches conflict in a collaborative manner. By engaging in this approach, the leader is leading in a more assertive manner versus an aggressive head-on manner to reach a team consensus. When the teammate has possession of the ball, she needs to control the play.

The team leader plays a major role in handling conflict effectively. For the soccer team, that leader is the team captain. For the USWNT team, that was Julie Foudy. One of the reasons she led her team so remarkably was because she handled conflict so well.

## 1:1 with Julie Foudy

Julie Foudy, teammate of Kristine's and co-captain of the US Women's National Soccer team, had 271 caps and was inducted into the National Soccer Hall of Fame in 2007. After her playing career, she was president of the Women's Sports Foundation, as well as the founder of the Julie Foudy Sports Leadership Academy. She is also an ESPN commentator for women's soccer telecasts, and author of *Choose to Matter*.

### Did the USWNT have constructive disagreement during your tenure as captain?

This team was successful because we trusted each other, believed in each other, and had a really positive team culture. We tried to create a team culture where everyone felt valued. That was essential. We understood that a player may be frustrated if they were not a starter, yet they need to channel that in a positive way. This environment was intentional and conscious, and generally prevented conflicts.

It helped that our coaches were good at listening and valued player input. Tony would say, "I heard you, thanks for sharing," and often reply, "But I did not change my mind." He would also ask for the pulse of the team; we had constant and open communication.

Finally, we found joy in what we were doing! Things can seem like such a big deal, but your team has to keep its sense of humor in order to handle the tough situations. Carla Overbeck was the best at this. At least once a game I would be screaming my head off, with my veins popping out, because I am ultracompetitive. Carla would look at me and start cracking up laughing with a "what are you doing?" That's how she diffused the situation, using humor on the field. At least once a game we were giggling. What I miss most about the team is the laughter.

## How did your team respond to conflict?

We were assertive; we had to be courageous in representing the team for what is right. We couldn't even comprehend equal pay at that time. We were the first generation of players, who were getting wiser over the years. We lost a lot of players who had to get a real job.

I reached out to tennis great Billie Jean King in 1995 when we were at a sports roundtable. About to sign a new contract with US Soccer, Billie Jean launched into a story about how women's tennis broke away, how scary it was, and what they did. She said, "You, the players, have to do this . . . take it by the horns!" We made the decision as a team to not sign the contract, which meant risking the opportunity to play in the Olympics. This was our lifelong dream that we were willing to risk in order to be treated fairly. We knew we were fighting for a better place for the next generation coming through.

This was a new territory for all of us, as we wanted to play in the first Olympics in which women's soccer was a sport. Our team had to be strong and show a united front. As captains, Carla and I knew we needed to set the tone for the team. The team trusted Carla Overbeck and myself, and we would have constant conference calls together to express concerns and provide a forum to voice concerns. When a player said, "I am scared," I would respond, "I am too, yet we have to stick together."

We got a new contract. We played in the 1996 Olympics. We won gold. Billie Jean was with us for years, always providing mentoring and advising. She was a godsend for our team.

### As USWNT captain, what did you do to mediate conflict?

I think our team always understood that the captains made decisions in the team's best interest. If we had outliers who were more concerned about their personal gain than the team's, we tried to bring them into the fold. We would hold an intervention to minimize the damage to the team and talk with the outlier player instead of taking it to the coach. We would sit down and have a conversation. Instead of going through all the things she did wrong, we explained to her what we needed and gave her a list of all the ways she could help the team. We would explain the situation so they could understand why we were making the decisions for the team. We would explain that self-interest does not trump what is in the best interest for the team. If we had allowed it to persist, it would have broken the soul of the team.

## Tactics for Your Team

Powerhouses must be able to handle conflict effectively. The first principle is a team should proactively address any issue by responding effectively. The second of these three principles is to disagree constructively, having a candid conversation with multiple perspectives to find an optimal solution. Finally, a team leader should mediate conflict by proactively addressing any issue in an assertive manner.

Consider how you can practice conflict resolution skills in your own organization. How will you:

1. Put the collective priorities and needs of the larger organization ahead of individual departments?

2. Engage openly in productive discussion around important issues?

3. Be assertive in addressing and resolving conflict?

## Pillar 4:

# MOTIVATE

Powerhouses are motivated to win, as the team members are energized about seeking to accomplish their goals together. Their team chemistry is a tight-knit bond that prompts greatness. Their team ethos inspires hard work, drive, and spark. This winning mentality galvanizes performance at the highest level.

*Kristine coached for three years as a volunteer assistant at The University of Texas. She was fortunate to have worked alongside her college teammate and friend Angela Kelly, and with assistant coaches Jaimel Johnson and Keeley Dowling. (Credit: The Lilly-Heavey Family)*

# Creating Team Chemistry

*"Worthwhile things are not built in short periods of time.*
*They come from a consistent series of actions."*

**—Angela Kelly**

The 1999 World Cup Final Game in front of over ninety thousand fans at the Rose Bowl in Pasadena was where Kristine's teammate, Brandi Chastain, scored the fifth and final goal for her team to beat China, a shot that would change their lives forever.

Brandi spontaneously took off her jersey in celebration and slid on her knees, flexing her arms with fists clenched. While this action is common in men's soccer, it was novel for a woman to celebrate sans jersey in a sports bra. The moment was captured in one of the most famous soccer photographs ever, featured on the covers of *Sports Illustrated*, *Time*, *Newsweek*, and newspapers around the world. Brandi described it as "momentary insanity, nothing more, nothing less. I wasn't thinking about anything. I thought, 'This is the greatest moment of my life on the soccer field.'"[42]

---

42  Chris Greenberg, "Brandi Chastain Goal Wins 1999 Women's World Cup, Triggers Iconic Celebration," Huffington Post.com, July 10, 2013, https://www.huffingtonpost.com/2013/07/10/brandi-chastain-goal-celebration-sports-bra_n_3576091.html.

The goal Brandi scored brought relief and complete happiness. Yet, it wasn't about Brandi and her individual achievement, although the magazine covers and interview requests would make you think otherwise. Brandi had a role, as did each of the twenty players on the USWNT. There were five who took and made their shots during this nail-biting shootout: Carla, Joy, Kristine, Mia, and of course Brandi. China's third shooter's shot was saved by the US's Hall of Fame goalkeeper, Briana Scurry. The team members were gathered at midfield when Brandi made her goal, and the photo of the team's ecstatic reaction to Brandi's shot is one of Kristine's favorites from all their game experiences.

Kristine also had her own critical play. Kristine's role on corner kicks was to stand on the goal line and cover the right post. She was positioned there because of the strength of her dominant left foot and because her teammates' height advantage was better for battling for headers in the penalty box. Of course, she could not use her hands. When China took their corner kick, Briana Scurry, the US goalkeeper, stretched out her hands but could not get to Yunjie's header on goal. In that split second, Kristine jumped and headed the ball off the goal line to keep the US in the game. Brandi reflected on the play, saying, "It is do or die because if the ball goes in the net, the game is over." She went on to describe Kristine's contributions, "It was a most incredible game. She did her job, taking care of the details that absolutely matter. She did exactly what she was supposed to do."

The team needed many crucial plays to get the overall win that day. The game consisted of ninety minutes of hard-fought regulation time and two fifteen-minute grueling overtimes. Still, neither team scored. The game was years of work by twenty women pushing each other to be the best. It was Coach Tony DiCicco's "I love my job" mentality. It was Cindy Parlow's goal versus Brazil in the semifinals to get the team to the championship game.

In short, it was a team putting the team first. Years of practice resulted in teammates knowing their role, pushing each other to be better, heading a ball off the line, making a key save in penalty kicks, tallying five penalty kicks, and most importantly—a team supporting one another because they all wanted to be the best in the world.

## Why Team Chemistry Is Important

The popular phrase "all for one and one for all" captures the camaraderie and shared spirit of teamwork. Each team member understands the character of the team. The workplace climate is conducive to exceptional work. This chemistry creates sparks. To create team chemistry, an organization should follow the principles of clarifying roles, building trust, and holding team members accountable.

# Clarify Roles

When roles are clarified, the possibilities of conflict are minimized because tasks are coordinated. People don't step on each other's toes or overstep their boundaries because they know how to work together.

Kristine captured the first principle to clarify roles when she reflected on the World Cup Championship in 1999 saying, "We all have our role, whatever it may be—coming off the bench, trainer, coach, or protecting the post on corner kicks. It all makes a difference."

# Specific Roles

To accomplish tasks, each team member needs to know their specific role. This is not about just understanding what they do; it is an understanding of *why* they do what they do and how they contribute to the larger mission and purpose of the team. Assigning tasks creates a clear expectation of role responsibility and job expectation in relation to the goals the group is trying to accomplish. Yale Divinity Professor H. E. Luccock captured this interdependence of roles when he said, "No one can whistle a symphony. It takes a whole orchestra to play it."[43]

This cross-functional understanding also provides purpose and motivation to the team members, and the team members know where to focus and prioritize their efforts. Instead of guessing what is important and being displeased with team workflow, they know what effort is required to accomplish which task. Coworkers need to understand what each person really does; otherwise, each team member does not understand how to most effectively work together. Once they complete their task, they need to support others executing their tasks. With this commitment to their team role, they are contributing to the team's success.

---

43  As quoted in Dianne Kirby, "No one can whistle a symphony. It takes an orchestra to play it," *Asian Social Science* 7, no. 4 (April 2011).

For example, most law firms are a pyramid with the partner at the top, followed by senior associates, associates, and paralegals. While the big dog at the top charges a hefty hourly rate, the partner is totally dependent on the research completed by associates and paralegals at the bottom of the pyramid. It is an ecosystem of interdependence where each team member knows their role.

## Strength-Based Roles

Each team member's role should be delegated based on their strengths, which will help a team to balance one member's weaknesses with another's strengths. These complementary skill sets, experiences, and personalities strengthen the team. For example, a team needs a strategic thinker as well as a team member who is strong in execution. Without both, the team is not as effective. With neither, the team is not as effective. Team members appreciate when their individual strengths are utilized to optimize team performance. Teamwork divides the task and multiplies success.

### A Note about Team Loafers

Structure provides a degree of mutual role accountability, as everyone knows their collective goal. On the flip side, a high-performing team will resent a free-riding member who does not meet their role expectations and is considered a "team loafer."

Anybody who has worked on a team has experienced a nonperforming team member giving minimal effort, and they can tell the story of how this has negatively impacted the team by creating an unfair amount of work picked up by the other team members. While team members can step in to cover for the team loafer, it's much better if everyone on the team does their part to avoid placing undue burden on any one member. Whether on a school project, a neighborhood committee, or in the workplace, leaders should not tolerate a team loafer.

## Engage the Twentieth Player

The USWNT was able to win the World Championship because twenty players knew their roles and trained to be the best in the world at them. Each player on the team believed that her role mattered, even though only eleven starters and three subs are allowed during each game. That means that six players, about one-third of the team, will not see the field during a game. How do those players stay engaged?

Coach Dorrance understood this challenge and actively labeled it as "engaging the twentieth player." Each team member understood that whether she was the star player or the twentieth player, whether she was a starter or a substitute, whether she scored on offense or played stout defense, her role mattered. The coach's focus on the twentieth player increased all players' buy-in and engagement, which impacted the team's reciprocity, cooperation, and ultimate success.

Business leaders, like Coach Dorrance, need to "engage the twentieth player" by identifying the desired team member behaviors to encourage and reward. Common business practices to encourage this cross-role understanding include job rotations, role shadowing, and cross-training. By proactively acknowledging desired team behaviors, in addition to having processes in place to develop understanding across roles, a team builds the needed role clarity to be effective.

# Trust

At Kristine's Hall of Fame induction, she said, "A team is stronger when you stick together on and off the field. Winning is easier together, and fighting for what is right is as well." When her UNC teammate Angela Kelly became the head coach of The University of Texas's women's soccer team in 2011, she had to change the team culture so that players trusted one another. She applied what she learned from Coach Dorrance at UNC as a player, as well as what she learned from women's basketball Coach Pat Summitt at the University of Tennessee, to create a winning, trusting team culture for the Texas team.

To encourage culture, Angela has a theme word for every soccer season, such as "grit," "family," or "courage" that she asks her players to focus on. In addition, she gives each player a book to read that conveys the season's principle. All of this is about changing the team members' mindset so that team members learn that the team is bigger than the self. While players resisted at first, the consistent approach, as well as the winning on the field, resulted in players buying into the concept. Now there is a culture at The University of Texas where the women soccer players trust each other and care more about the success of the team instead of just individual success.

## Build Trust

In a knowledge-sharing economy, trust among team members is essential. The level of trust is related to the quality of the relationships team members share. When you achieve trust, your team members' behavior becomes predictable. You have faith in their competence, and they rise to meet your expectations. This progression of trust building greatly depends on the way in which the team is originally composed, under what circumstances the team members get to know each other, and how the team coordinates their efforts to meet their shared goals. The trusting relationship is dependent not only on each team member, but also on the organization's overall culture.[44]

When a team's work objective requires high interdependence, such as working on a high-profile project for a client, trust is critical for performance, since it is a precursor to the necessary collaboration between respective expertise and roles. You could say the amount of trust required on a team is directly correlated with the collaboration required to accomplish the task. With trust among team members, people are more willing to help each other. Also, when the inevitable conflict arises, it's much easier to reconcile.

Trust building is the foundation for an individual's success on any team, yet these deeper relationships require intentional effort and time. You cannot lock individuals in a room for five days and expect a team to emerge. So, start now and work on building trust in your own organization and teams. There are typically three factors present when developing trust, which are benevolence, reliability, and honesty.

---

44  Xusen Cheng, Guopeng Yin, Aida Azadegan, and Gwendolyn Kolfschoten, "Trust Evolvement in Hybrid Team Collaboration: A Longitudinal Case Study," *Group Decision and Negotiation* 25, no. 2 (May 2015), https://www.researchgate.net/publication/277352784_Trust_Evolvement_in_Hybrid_Team_Collaboration_A_Longitudinal_Case_Study.

## Encourage Benevolence

When a team member has confidence that his well-being or something that he cares about will be protected, that illustrates benevolence. When someone joins a team, try to start a friendly relationship. A minimal degree of trust and inclusion are necessary for new teammates or work colleagues to open up and confide in another, as you have to help them recognize and accept that level of risk. You can help establish mutual respect by praising each teammate in front of others.

## Foster Reliability

Team members are considered reliable when they have competent, predictable, and consistent behavior. Research shows this improves team members' willingness to increase their efforts.[45] A team member should be confident that their teammate will meet expectations and that their knowledge, skills, abilities, capacity, and resources will enable them to perform as expected. You can foster a culture of reliability by reminding your colleagues or team members of the tasks you have completed as you progress to your goal. Encourage all coworkers to keep their word and to work hard for the benefit of the team.

This reliability also determines the willingness of a team member to exchange knowledge with other team members for the benefit of the team performance and organization. You share relevant information to test assumptions and inferences.

## Honesty

When a team member is honest, they display good character, integrity, and authenticity. As your team shares more and communicates, the team's trust will grow with each new experience. Discussing these shared experiences will help coworkers further understand the other person's motives. In these conversations, teammates can share personal and relevant information without withholding facts that are critical. The team member is vulnerable, allowing her

---

45  Xusen Cheng, Guopeng Yin, Aida Azadegan, and Gwendolyn Kolfschoten, "Trust Evolvement in Hybrid Team Collaboration: A Longitudinal Case Study," *Group Decision and Negotiation* 25, no. 2 (May 2015), https://www.researchgate.net/publication/277352784_Trust_Evolvement_in_Hybrid_Team_Collaboration_A_Longitudinal_Case_Study.

colleagues to see her weaknesses, addressing her mistakes, and even by admitting when she is unsure of something by saying, "I don't know."

## Value of Trust

Teamwork requires interdependence, where the interest of one party cannot be achieved without relying upon another. This is most critical when results are created jointly in a highly interactive environment. The team member feels secure in her job and comfortable with her team members. The organization, in turn, respects the team's contributions, and the team has deep confidence in the business sustainability. With an honest environment, team members value and support one another. These teams are able to overcome conflicts and misunderstandings even as they openly disagree.

Team trust is dynamic and fragile. You must consider the team foundation that enhances or diminishes the development of trusting team members.

## Accountability

UNC has a set of core values that are the cultural foundation of their soccer program, designed as a platform for the players to reach their potential. These behavior principles produce extraordinary results. The rising seniors meet to discuss how they can live these and drive the program culture. The values are only meaningful if these senior leaders embrace them and demonstrate acceptable behavior.

The team's values include the following descriptors: tough, disciplined, focused, relentless, resilient, positive, classy, caring, noble, selfless, galvanizing, and grateful. Players decided to add a thirteenth value to this character-building institutional list, "accountability." They paraphrased ManU's manager Sir Alex Ferguson when they told the team, "We want to take responsibility for our own actions, our own errors, our own performance level, and eventually for every result."

It is the individual's obligation to the team to do their job. Accountability is this external commitment to the team.

## Team Accountability and Personal Responsibility

A powerhouse has a strong sense of accountability between dependable team members to achieve their stretch goals. Individual team members feel the responsibility that they have for the team. The collective goal is clear, and all team members are aligned.

When you are part of a powerhouse, you respect the process and follow through on your commitments to the team. The leaders hold the team members accountable for the results. When a team member fails to contribute per their role, the team calls them out for that inaction or negative behavior. And it is on the team member to own up to these expectations and course correct. The internal commitment to oneself for getting the job done is responsibility. USWNT Coach Tony DiCicco reinforced this principle when he coached, saying, "Placing blame on others is easy. Taking responsibility for yourself is empowering."[46]

As an example, a manufacturing company developed team accountability across thousands of employees in global facilities. To do this, they evaluated teamwork maturity on a four-level scale and found that as teamwork evolved, so did the type of leadership. On the low end with weaker teamwork accountability, the team required more command and control leadership. As the teamwork effectiveness improved, the leadership became more agile, and the team was more empowered.

Before this team empowerment, they would not look upstream or downstream to see the impacts of their actions on the overall manufacturing process. Now with a team who is accountable, they are effectively working across industrial engineering, commercial, research, support functions, maintenance, and mold manufacturing to improve the effectiveness of their production process. By evaluating teamwork maturity and focusing on accountability, they have improved their overall business performance.

## Carry Your Own Weight

Accountability for exceptional quality between team members increases the standard of excellence. Team members do not want to be the weak link, so they continuously push themselves and encourage one other to perform at higher

---

46  Tony DiCicco, Colleen Hacker, *Catch Them Being Good* (New York: Penguin Books, 2002).

levels. When you have accountability, everyone carries their own weight to accomplish the team goal. This self-directed higher ambition and energy level raises the bar for everyone on the team. The team has sustained commitment to their stretch goals that set the high standard. When this significant outcome is a success, it is celebrated, which pushes the standard even higher. Your team enters into a league of its own.

The University of Texas women's soccer Coach Angela Kelly learned these powerhouse team principles to create team chemistry in order to build a successful collegiate soccer program.

# 1:1 with Coach Angela Kelly

Coach Kelly was a teammate of Kristine's at UNC from 1990–1992. During her time at UNC, Angela won ninety-seven games, lost one game, and tied one, while collecting four national championships. Before becoming the women's soccer head coach at The University of Texas, she spent twelve successful years building the Tennessee Lady Vols soccer program into a perennial championship contender, where she was mentored by the legendary women's basketball coach, Pat Summitt. Angela also played on the Canadian National Team for nine years, including the 1995 World Cup, and was the third woman to be enshrined into the Canadian Soccer Hall of Fame in 2004.

## How did you learn the importance of clarifying roles?

After I played at UNC, Coach Dorrance encouraged me to get into the coaching profession. I took the assistant coach position at the University of Tennessee. I had just played in the 1995 World Cup in Sweden for the Canadian team and was preparing for the 1996 Olympics when the head coach position opened up.

Coach Pat Summitt, one of the most successful basketball coaches in history, called me into her office and inquired about my intentions about becoming the head coach. When I shared that, in my mind, I could keep practicing with the team so that I could represent Canada and then play professionally, she responded, "You do not play soccer anymore, you coach now. Do you understand your new role?" In that one minute, I was now the coach of a big-time program! My new role as the Lady Vol coach set me on an incredible path. Coach Summitt clarified my role at a critical juncture in my life.

## Why is trust important on a team?

I brought Kristine to The University of Texas to be a volunteer assistant coach for the women's soccer team in 2014. She brought presence, as one of the most storied players in the world. She had the humility to train collegiate players who were in awe of her—she just wanted to make them better. They grasped her competitive drive, which is what I saw back when Kristine and I played together.

Back when we were playing North Carolina State in the NCAA semifinals, my legs felt numb to me during warm-ups because I was so full of anxiety. Kristine approached me and said, "Trust in us. We will do this together. Don't worry about anything. Refocus and get ready to go!"

Just like I trusted Kristine when we played together, I trusted her when we coached together. With her and my other coaches, trust builds over time. Worthwhile things are not built in short periods of time. They come from a consistent series of actions. Our staff works *with* me, not *for* me. Our coaching staff needs chemistry, as we spend a lot of time together. We are invested in each other's lives and loyal to each other. That investment of time in a relationship goes a long way. Successful programs have longevity of the staff—continuity, loyalty, and consistency—because they've been built on the foundation of trust.

## How did you learn accountability?

At my first athletics department meeting at the University of Tennessee, there were twenty-three sports represented. Coach Pat Summitt asked, "Who in here has won four national championships?" Being brand new, I sheepishly put up my hand, and she said, "Meet me in my office after this meeting." Coach Summitt, who could be the Tennessee governor if she were still alive, had a presence unlike any other, commanding a standing ovation when she walked into the basketball arena from *both* teams.

Unsure of what to expect after the meeting, I went to her office. Summitt told me that we were going to be friends. That relationship grew until I became the head coach, and the athletic director formally made Coach Summitt my mentor. Summitt moved my office to the basketball arena and made sure that I checked in with her every day. I made sure I was in my office before she got there and stayed until after she left. We played golf together, had our dogs play together, and I was at her home so much, I became her son's big sister. She was willing to share all her wisdom, yet she held me accountable.

She had the highest standard for how she operated. You go all in or you don't go at all with her. She was willing to put her neck on the line for something that she believed in, without worrying about the repercussions.

I and everyone else had the highest level of respect for her. Professionally, she gave me so much strength. Coach Summitt worked her butt off to make sure that Tennessee women's basketball succeeded. She is at the forefront of women's athletics, and a big reason why every female in America has more opportunities today. I am most grateful for this relationship, as she is like a second mother to me.

## Tactics for Your Team

To be effective, a powerhouse needs chemistry. They create this by clarifying roles and engaging every player on the team. They also achieve chemistry by building trust from being benevolent, reliable, and honest in team relationships. Finally, they demand accountability.

Take a moment to consider the following to see how you can create chemistry in your own organization. How will you:

1. Clarify roles, responsibilities, tasks, processes, and dependencies?

2. Build team trust?

3. Hold team members accountable to commitments?

.

*"There is nothing like walking around the Rose Bowl as world champions with teammates and friends like Tisha Venturini-Hoch and Cindy Parlow,"* Kristine said. *"It was an honor to wear the USA jersey and represent my country for twenty-three years." (Credit: John Todd/isiphotos.com)*

# Cultivating the Team Ethos

*"Everyone brings their part and puts the puzzle together.*
*When you come together perfectly,*
*then you win championships."*

**—Tisha Venturini-Hoch**

Today, Kristine runs a soccer camp called TeamFirst Soccer Academy with Mia Hamm and Tisha Venturini-Hoch, her friends and soccer teammates. The TeamFirst Soccer Academy is dedicated to providing girls and young women an opportunity to develop as individual players within a disciplined and unselfish team environment. The academy strives to encourage players to respect the integrity of the game while it continues to nurture the players' love for soccer.

Many of the values that Kristine and her teammates learned from playing the game at UNC and USWNT are now being paid forward to the next generation of players. This soccer camp travels around the country to teach kids not only about soccer but also about how to be a better player and person, showing young athletes their passion and love for the game. Mia, Tisha, and Kristine have cultivated a team who all believe in this message, one that is consistent and demonstrated through their staff.

Note, their soccer academy is not called "Mia Hamm's Soccer Academy" or "Kristine's Kicks" or "Tisha's Technical and Tactical Soccer." The three women wanted to fuel the principle of placing the team first. Yes, there are individual awards. As a collegiate junior, Kristine won the Hermann Trophy, awarded annually by the Missouri Athletic Club to the United States' top male and female college soccer players. Mia and Tisha won the same trophy in subsequent years. Yet, in spite of these individual accolades, when they were naming their soccer academy they held firm to their core strategy of putting their team identity first. Only then can the team be greater than the sum of the parts.

Coach Dorrance reminded them during their years of playing soccer together, "We play for each other."[47] This was their guiding principle for decades. This focus on teamwork is what led to their team's dynamic success, and it continues to this day. Or as Kristine reflects, "If you care about the people you work with, then you work harder."

## Why Ethos Is Important

Cultivating a team ethos is pivotal in the corporate world. An ethos is the guiding character of an organization, its reputation. A corporate ethos exists, whether a leader engages to create it or not. This ethos is the essence, character, and spirit of the team, manifested in their beliefs and aspirations, and it creates a team climate.

Although many companies talk about their culture, only a few are proactive at creating it. For most, they do not work to define and cultivate the ethos that they want, and end up with one that they do not want. To intentionally build an ethos, norms, standards, and shared values should be clearly communicated so that all team members understand the operating rules they need to uphold. Culture leads to commitment, and ultimately, performance. The team ethos comes down to three principles: build friendships, increase self-awareness, and develop team awareness.

---

47  Peter Tollman, Josh Serlin, Michelle Akers, Anson Dorrance, "The Power of Inspiration, Perspiration, and Cooperation—in Sports and in Business," The Boston Consulting Group, June 13, 2018, https://www.bcg.com/publications/2018/power-inspiration-perspiration-cooperation-sports-business.aspx.

# Build Friendships

An aspect of cultivating team ethos is building friendships among team members. There are many social aspects to work. The human interactions that teamwork requires include building rapport, communicating, managing conflict, and facilitating problem solving. The foundation for these interactions is the friendship team members share with each other. These friendships grow over common experiences, shared meaning, and successful task completions. Individuals think of the "we" part of work instead of "I" or "us versus them."

During Kristine's Hall of Fame induction speech, she said, "Relationships outlast the game of soccer. When I think about what I remember the most about playing, it isn't the wins and losses—although they still feel good or still sting a bit—it is the people. It is the people that made my career so special." Among the people she is referring to are Mia and Tisha, but also many, many more friends. Over her twenty-three years on the USWNT, Kristine has had too many teammates to count; however, the experiences with those friends are what make her memories so valuable. Even though they live all over the world today, she and her former teammates still have strong bonds and travel to see each other. Their teammate "friendship" remains, even though they are not competing on the field anymore. These friendships have led to joint businesses, collegiate coaching jobs, and many other ventures. One such example of how these friendships have led to more opportunity is the 1:1 interviews throughout this book. Each person we asked to speak with made themselves immediately available for Kristine. The game may have brought Kristine and her teammates together, but their friendships keep them together.

## Supportive Professionals

In the knowledge economy, business problems have become more volatile, uncertain, complex, and ambiguous. Friendship creates a psychological safety net where a team member feels confident to contribute without fear of retribution or exclusion. These team members, in turn, take risks, share opinions, and display emotions, because they feel free (and safe) enough to bring their whole self to the team. Through candid conversations, team members understand others' thoughts and feelings. Paying attention to the friendships on a team impacts the team's productivity, innovation, and individual satisfaction. Team trust is higher when there are high-quality friendships with mutual respect, accountability, and advice seeking. These types of friendships create a productive bond and a psychological safety net.

Research shows that workplace teams composed of friends who hold each other to high standards perform better than teams that are only made up of acquaintances. These friends communicate in a fluid and thorough manner, with a common understanding of each other's background experiences.[48] This candid communication is especially productive when the focus is on maximizing output—which is what most businesses are trying to do, and what Kristine and her teammates did on the soccer field. The reason for this, similar to Kristine's team, is that friends can coordinate tasks more effectively. They know each other's strengths as well as weaknesses. Based on this knowledge, they have a deeper understanding on how to most effectively delegate the required tasks in order to complete the work most efficiently.

## True Colors

Individuals want a colleague who cares, is sincere, and is genuine. Team members may not become best friends with a work colleague; however, a strong relationship can exist for support when challenges surface. This foundation of a team helps colleagues come together and work through complex problems. Think of the calm and critically important reactions of emergency room nurses and physicians during life-critical events, the high pressure environment of employees as they push to close sales during the last week of the quarter, or the intense response of teammates during a high-pressure World Cup championship game. In these stressful situations, who your team member really is comes out—their true colors—rather than the image they portray to be during normal times. With a solid foundation of friendship, you know who they are and are confident in how they will respond when it is time for your team's critical performance.

On the soccer field, a player receives a yellow card as a warning after they have committed an offense. If a more serious offense foul occurs, the player is dismissed with a red card. While a business leader doesn't carry yellow and red cards in her pocket, she does need to give candid feedback to team members when their behavior is out of bounds. The friendships that she has

---

48  "Teamwork and Friendship Mix Well," *Industrial and Systems Engineering at Work* 50, no. 2 (February 2018).

developed with her employees allow her to give out these critiques without derailing the team's momentum.

For many, these relationships can benefit you even after you leave a company. It is a network to share industry and vendor information. The trust built while working together at a company lasts, and you turn to those friendships when looking for industry information or advice in your current job. These relationships can also lead to future jobs down the road. While a resume is important, having someone who vouches for your previous working experience can help you land a new job even faster.

## Celebrate and Laugh

Does your team enthusiastically celebrate its wins? When someone gets a new client, new product development, or hits a sales goal, do you celebrate? Unfortunately, the answer is "no" for too many people. This lack of shared joy in achievement can hinder your team's ethos.

USWNT Captain Julie Foudy, recalling the 1996 team winning Olympic gold, said, "When we got on the field we were very intense, but off the field we were always pulling pranks and messing around. The year before, we had talent on the team, but we didn't have the joy or the unity."[49] The friendship between the players propelled them the extra mile they needed to capture the gold. The strong bonds that allowed them to "play" with each other as friends in the locker room and beyond developed a close ethos that propelled them to excellence. To strengthen your team, be sure to celebrate individual as well as collective achievements—and to keep your sense of humor.

Humor can help break down walls and help build teams; however, it can also be divisive when used in a reckless manner that can be misinterpreted. Note that this playful nature is not at a team member's expense—it is not putting one person down for others to have a laugh. If a team member does poke fun, it is usually self-deprecating. Also, in diverse workplaces and global teams, what is funny to one group can be very hurtful for others. Remember, inappropriate remarks that are an attempt to be humorous can backfire and be used against you.

---

49  Peter Tollman, Josh Serlin, Michelle Akers, Anson Dorrance, "The Power of Inspiration, Perspiration, and Cooperation—in Sports and in Business," The Boston Consulting Group, June 13, 2018, https://www.bcg.com/publications/2018/power-inspiration-perspiration-cooperation-sports-business.aspx.

# Increase Self-Awareness

Self-awareness is the degree to which a person knows and understands themselves. It helps leaders, and their teams, be in control of the situation.

Coach Dorrance said, "The first step in player development is for the player to figure out who she is."[50] He asked his players what their goals were for the year, both on the soccer field and in the university classroom, and encouraged all of them to set higher expectations. He wanted to understand each team member's "internal narrative," which included the self-beliefs that both motivated and inhibited them as a person and a player. To do this, he asked each player to rank themselves on a 1 to 5 scale on such attributes as self-discipline, competitive fire, self-belief, love of playing the game, love of watching the game, and grit. This assessment not only helped him, it helped them as players and people to gain a deeper level of self-awareness. As he said, "A great way to unlock potential is to get the player as close to the truth of her internal narrative as possible."

A worker's personal story can impact the team's work performance. For Kristine's team members who were not starters, or those who got subbed out, they needed to have an inner discussion to make a choice on "how to be." One of Kristine's teammates had to deal with a different adversity when she was a starter for years and then became a reserve and was not happy about it. She had to decide if it was going to be about her or if it was going to be about the team. She had a positive attitude during the transformation in her new role, thus serving as a perfect example on how to be a good teammate. She literally put the team first and stepped aside for the greater good of the team.

## Personal Narratives

A lack of self-awareness or an inability to seek positivity in one's personal story in the workplace can be problematic—not just for that particular person, but for all of their workplace team, as their relationship with their self will have a direct impact on how they relate with others. If a colleague gets caught with a "woe is me" attitude, it will drain the energy of the entire team. Surprisingly,

---

50  Peter Tollman, Josh Serlin, Michelle Akers, Anson Dorrance, "The Power of Inspiration, Perspiration, and Cooperation—in Sports and in Business," The Boston Consulting Group, June 13, 2018, https://www.bcg.com/publications/2018/power-inspiration-perspiration-cooperation-sports-business.aspx.

many are not aware of their negative contributions to dysfunctional team behavior and the unintended consequences of their unpleasant behavior. Your team should be equipped to take and give feedback with each other so team members become aware of their behavior's unintended consequences. If you are not aware of your own blind spots, then you lose credibility, trust, and respect from your team members.

As a leader, your role is to help employees with their internal narrative like Coach Dorrance did for his players. A leader helps team members build their self-awareness through ongoing constructive feedback in every work situation that they encounter. During these 1:1 discussions, a leader also can address a negative attitude and possibly remove the cause so the team member overcomes these obstacles in order to unlock their full potential. Of course, this improves the overall team performance, which is the ultimate goal of the leader.

## Reflect

Knowing yourself is not a new concept; however, many people struggle to develop this critical component of emotional intelligence. To better develop your self-awareness, you must take time to reflect. Many businesspeople go straight from meeting to meeting, from one email to another, and from one work deliverable to the next without taking time to reflect.

By taking time to stop and pause, think about their activity, consider how they performed, or how their performance or interactions affected others, these individuals could improve themselves and their teams. Introspection and reflection enable individuals to know when and how their actions have positively or negatively affected the team.

To be effective, you must be honest and candid with your introspection and you must do it often. Basically, whenever there is a failure, you must hypothesize what you could have done differently to better serve the needs of the situation (and team) and not yourself. You must, to the best of your ability, put yourself in the other person's cleats in order to observe your behavior without prejudices.

For maximum benefit, you will need to assert your strengths in the appropriate circumstances, as well as not asserting your weaknesses inappropriately. We all have our "blind spots," which are disparities between self-reported skills and peer ratings. Basically, they are false understandings of yourself. If you do not explore these areas, you will not understand your negative impact on team members and remain unaware of your limitations and imperfections.

Based on your self-reflection and this constructive self-criticism, you can actively adjust, redirect, and reshape your behavior. With continued practice, you can self-monitor your work and presentation to others so that you are regulating your progress, which will help you achieve greater things. Through self-appraisal and social team member comparison, you can also learn how you are perceived within your team and company. Once you have a good awareness of this, you will be in touch with how these factors influence and anchor your decisions, behavior, and language. You will also understand how they drive your attitudes, intentions, moods, mental state, needs, and emotions.

## Celebrate You!

This self-appraisal assists you in having a deeper understanding of your unique traits. Each of us has differences in thinking, feeling, and behaving. There is a popular saying, "Celebrate you!" You should be confident in your abilities to create results and affect your team through serving them. Once you have a clear view of your value, you can choose your work assignments so they play to your strengths, and not overcommit to something that you are not capable of completing. You can be authentic and take responsibility during a failure to learn from mistakes.

Being on a team enables you to grow as a person. Building your self-awareness of your strengths and weaknesses will help you best contribute to the team. One of Michael Jackson's most famous songs is "Man in the Mirror," where he discusses the importance of becoming self-aware and changing your behavior to make the world a better place. When you develop your self-awareness, you do not stop making errors. Instead, you have an increased capacity to learn from those moments when you fall down. When's the last time you took a look in the proverbial mirror?

## Team-Awareness

Your own self-awareness helps build your team-awareness, as you have a large impact on others. When you work beyond individual self-interests to put the team's interests above individual, self-serving interests, you'll have developed team-awareness. This means you'll understand the team's strengths, weaknesses, and abilities. Kristine's teammate Megan Rapinoe said, "You have to be selfless, but you can't lose yourself in that. You need to know what you personally contribute as an individual." By knowing where you fit in the team's network of skills and weaknesses, you can optimize your contributions.

On the soccer field, the game is all about team positioning and movement. Players are constantly moving without the ball—they only touch the ball a small percentage of the game. This requires effective team-awareness. Good teams have players who are aware of their positions, as well as the other players' positions, and they change their movements based on what the other team is doing. During the match, they must know their teammates well to anticipate where they will move in a specific situation so they know where they can pass the ball.

Team-awareness includes attention to detail, knowledge of a player's strengths, and team optimization. When you are team-aware, you will know where the player is strong, as well as where they are not. For example, you wouldn't pass the ball in the air to a teammate who was not confident in receiving a high ball, or to someone's right side if she was left-footed. Brazilian soccer player Pele, who some consider the greatest men's player of all time, understands the importance of team-awareness. He once said, "I am constantly being asked about individuals. The only way to win is as a team. Football is not about one or two or three star players."[51] And like an effective soccer team, your business team needs to operate with the awareness that it works best as a cohesive unit that puts individual interests aside for the better of the team.

## Improve Team Performance

Teamwork in business enables you to develop as a person and to build your team-awareness. When you feel truly known and valued, and not like you're just a cog in the wheel, then your team performance improves. As in sports, in business you must know your teammates well so you can effectively position yourself based on external circumstances, such as your peers' actions, what your competition is doing, and other environmental factors. To build team-awareness is to build empathy, flexibility, and social sensitivity in all types of work situations. This significantly impacts job performance in many

---

51 "About Us," Pelé Soccer, accessed February 2, 2019, https://pelesoccer.com/pages/about.

situations," including knowing what's in the best interest of the overall business rather than a specific department.

## Know Minds and Hearts

To build team-awareness, the first stage is understanding the mind. This includes knowing team members' perspectives, opinions, and logic. Each team member has a different view on the situation, and to understand their lens will help you know how they interpret their surroundings. In addition, it's important to know your team members' skills and behaviors, their working habits, individual personalities, and thinking styles. A good team member assesses others' body language and tone. They observe physical placement with the team, such as whether a team member is in the circle participating or standing outside the circle alone and not included.

After you understand the minds of your team members, the next stage is to know their hearts—their feelings, emotions, thoughts, and beliefs. Ideally, colleagues will understand your wants, needs, and expectations. This takes considerable time and effort, as it is making the invisible visible. Learn to listen to the words they use and observe the behaviors they choose. A team member should acknowledge when others support them by sharing their experience and expertise. Get the most out of your team members by showing a caring relationship.

One global company's chief financial officer was investing a huge financial amount in a new technology that would aggregate all the company's data into one "source of truth" location. He said he was attempting to standardize the company's processes. His goal for this large project was that instead of the company's people "working without thinking," that the technology would improve the processes so everyone would have the time to "think before working." He wanted his team to reflect, in order to improve teamwork and business outcomes. This CFO saw that today's work pace and pressure do not leave time to build team-awareness, and he strove to do something about it.

## Be Open to Feedback

To build on your self-reflection, invest in ongoing professional development, and be open to candid feedback from your colleagues and managers. In fact, actively seek constructive criticism to see how you can improve your own performance. One professional follows this advice by frequently asking those around him, "How can I perform better?" and "How can I be a better teammate?" He asked it so often, many colleagues responded with, "I knew you would ask me that question, so I thought about it ahead of time to share with you."

Team members should always be wondering how they can create more knowledge for the team while also expanding their own personal knowledge. If you are the team leader, think about how you can create a culture of feedback so all team members continuously learn to improve their performance. Many companies invest in training programs, one-on-one coaching, or 360-degree feedback assessments that compare/contrast your self-perspective with the perspective of a manager, peers, and direct reports. We also recommend implementing a regular feedback session with your team. This is time for solicited feedback on individual behaviors that affect the team, both positively and negatively, from the large actions to the small habits.

Tisha Venturini-Hoch was a huge part of the team ethos at UNC, USWNT, and now together again with Kristine at TeamFirst. In the interview that follows, you will see how healthy team relationships were crucial on all of her high-performing teams.

## 1:1 with Tisha Venturini-Hoch

Tisha Venturini-Hoch is no stranger to teamwork. Tisha played soccer with Kristine at UNC, where she won four national championships, and with the USWNT, where she won an Olympic gold medal in 1996. She also was a world champion with the 1999 FIFA World Cup. In 2010 she cofounded the TeamFirst Soccer Academy with Mia Hamm and Kristine Lilly.

### How do your friendships impact teamwork?

When I was a freshman at UNC, I was overwhelmed. I was straight from California, homesick, and not sure of my college decision. At a team dinner on Franklin Street one night, my insecurity of not feeling like I was a part of the team came to a head. I quickly ran out of the restaurant without any team members noticing, and I sat down across the street. Kristine was sitting next to me a minute later. She was a college junior, and she shared how hard it had been on her during her freshman year to be away from home, how she overcame being homesick, and how she overcame her insecurities about being on the team. She let me know that team members are paying attention and that they did care.

During the first women's World Cup in 1991, our two best players left the UNC team for the USWNT: Mia Hamm and Kristine. Coach Dorrance sat me down and told me that I needed to take over the game and score the goals we needed to become the national champions. He went on to say I would be the MVP. Most people don't think very much of themselves until someone else believes in you. That's what Coach Dorrance did for me. I ate up every word he said. He could get me to do anything because of the belief he instilled in me! I'm happy to say that we won the national championship.

My freshman year started off with being homesick and ended with being a national champion. It just goes to show that when you enjoy the people you are working with and care deeply for them, what you are doing becomes so much better.

## Share how teamwork relies on increasing one's self-awareness.

People bring different things to the table, so knowing what you are good at and doing it to the best of your ability is key. Every person should know their role. You should like it and contribute or move somewhere else.

Everyone brings their part and puts the puzzle together. When you come together perfectly, then you win championships. If you get out of your specialty, then the team won't be as effective. At different times of your career, you'll have different strengths and weaknesses. As you get older, you get slower. You have to have a positive attitude and no ego. You need to put the team before yourself. The team has a common goal and then has fun along the way.

When we were playing Santa Clara, on a road trip in California, we were losing at halftime. I had not lost a game at UNC, nor had we ever been behind at halftime. I was not going to lose that day, either. I had a crazy idea to bond the team together by wrapping athletic tape around our pinkie fingers. It had no performance purpose. It was just a team togetherness concept. I told the team, "Tape your pinkie. Get it on, now!" Silly, yes. Team bonding, yes. Did we win the game? Yes. The pinkie-taping tradition continued and actually lasted for years after I left. All you need in life is a positive attitude and pinkie tape!

## How did you have team-awareness?

In 1999, I went from a starter to a reserve player on the USWNT. Obviously, when you don't get the promotion you want, you think "dang." In my case, I wanted to play and was not happy about being taken off the field. But, if I had said, "This sucks," then I would have been gone.

Instead, I looked at the big picture, and I was in awe of my team. I realized I was lucky to be there. I knew what was expected of me, and then I had to say "yes" and accept my role. I have something that I can bring to the table to help the team be successful even if it is not the role I originally wanted. Coach DiCicco knew I would be important to the team winning because of how I fit with the others, and he also knew that I could bring out the best in other team members. My role was to be positive for the team and the other reserves, and have the bench ready to play. It comes down to attitude so you can do the best that you can for the team.

Every coach, leader, and player on the team made me feel valued. Starters would talk to the reserves a lot, and talk about how much they needed them. People above you make you feel needed and worthy. Coach DiCicco made every player feel important, from the top to the bottom of the roster. If you are not feeling it, then you are not going to get what you need from that person. Coach DiCicco was a genius in how he put that team together, as it was so special. Selecting one wrong team member could have ruined it. Every member of the 1999 team cared deeply for each other, and that extended to the coaching staff, security detail, massage therapists, and so forth. We were there for each other, first and foremost. We respected each other and really enjoyed playing together. We will forever be connected, much after when our soccer careers are over.

When I did get the opportunity to go into the game against North Korea in the World Cup, I scored two goals. After I scored one of my goals, I did a roundoff back flip!

# Tactics for Your Team

Teams need to cultivate a team ethos. To do this, team members need to build friendships, increase self-awareness, and develop team-awareness. Friendships are important to have on the team, as this creates a healthy bond and psychological safety net for team players. Increased self-awareness comes by knowing yourself. Team-awareness is also important so that individual members of the team can understand how they are perceived by others while also focusing on the specific dynamics within team relationships.

Take a moment to consider the following three principles as they apply to your own organization. How will you:

**1.** Develop relationships that enhance the team's dynamics?

**2.** Help team members become aware of their strengths, weaknesses, and others' perceptions of them?

**3.** Optimize team performance by knowing and leveraging each person's complementary strengths?

*Leading a team isn't always easy, and it is important to come together and regroup during games. Kristine wears the captain's armband, but the team worked together to be the best. This gathering on the field was during an international friendly at the Edward Jones Dome in St. Louis on October 13, 2007. (Credit: Bill Barrett/isiphotos.com)*

# Seizing a Winning Mentality

*"The objective in any team sport is to transform the group
from a mere collection of talented individuals
into a highly cohesive unit so that the whole
is greater than the sum of its parts."*

**—Dr. Colleen Hacker**

Each time Kristine goes on the field, she plans on winning. Every time. She doesn't like to lose. Every game mattered to her; even a "friendly" game's outcome impacted the impression of her team. The USWNT's stringent performance circumstances meant that each game had a significant consequence. The question for Kristine and her team was how to respond when they did not meet their goal. Kristine's motto is "always believe," which to her means, "You should never give up!" To do this, you need to get over your setbacks so that you do not stop growing, developing, or performing. You have to propel onward and upward. This requires a mental resilience to respond to opposition and failure.

Mia Hamm once said, "Kristine set the standard for the women's national team. She had one of the strongest mentalities of any player I played with; if there was something she wanted to accomplish, she just made her mind up and made it happen."[52] Coach Tony DiCicco, who coached her for 130 games with the USWNT as well as with the Boston Breakers of Women's Professional Soccer, said, "In all those years, I don't think I ever saw her have a bad game."[53] He mentions how she was always the hardest worker and the fittest player on every team she played for. A player's fitness increased team members' trust, because a fit player was able to give more effort on the field, be more reliable in a game, and be strong mentally. Late in her career, when Coach DiCicco would run fitness tests for the team, she was outperforming players almost half her age.

## Why a Winning Mentality Is Important

Powerhouses are in it to win it! They each have a certain quality that many try to emulate. Michael Jordan, National Basketball Association megastar, once said, "Talent wins games, but teamwork and intelligence wins championships."[54]

Your winning mentality is based on a strong and passionate work ethic. When you seize a winning mentality, you seek results. You want to make a difference. You go the extra mile to accomplish more. You always strive to achieve, even when the odds are against you. When you have a winning attitude, you have the confidence and mental agility to outperform your competition. Winning comes down to your mentality, and specifically seeking excellence, investing in teamwork satisfaction, and being resilient.

## Seek Excellence

Kristine's team had to buy in and believe in what the coach wanted them to do. If they weren't all in, then they wouldn't be successful. This standard of excellence is the motivation to strive to be the best, to have a competitive spirit, and to display an unrelenting passion for the work. It was Mia Hamm's attention to

52  Wayne Coffey, "Kristine Lilly, after a quarter-century of soccer brilliance, walks away from the game at age 39," NYDaily News, Jan. 22, 2011, https://www.nydailynews.com/sports/more-sports/kristine-lilly-quarter-century-soccer-brilliance-walks-game-age-39-article-1.150722.

53  Ibid.

54  Grant Freeland, "Talent Wins Games, Teamwork Wins Championships," Forbes.com, June 1, 2018, https://www.forbes.com/sites/grantfreeland/2018/06/01/talent-wins-games-teamwork-wins-championships/#5cd25cd64c8f.

detail in dribbling exercises through cones, Brandi Chastain's constant penalty kick practice, and Carli Lloyd's intentional training on long-distance shooting that contributed to these players' highest performance level.

Early in her career, Kristine had a sideline conversation with Coach Dorrance that not only shaped her career but also the rest of her life. After a training session in late December, he explained to her that he was not happy about some of the players' preparation for camp, saying, "The players are not fit." Her quick response was, "It's the holidays." To that, he replied, "Fitness has to be better. Fitness has to be a part of your life." At that moment, she learned how important fitness was to her coach. It was a standard of excellence they all needed to aspire toward. From then on, Kristine was determined to always be one of the fittest players on the team. Over time, she realized that adhering to that standard of fitness excellence would sustain her career's longevity.

Athletes strive for perfection during competition and try to not let moments of imperfection get in their way. This attitude and behavior encompass a high level of hope. Athletes put themselves out there and play on the edge of their game. They are also surrounded by their team's support. It is not a "just getting by" mentality that avoids failure. When they do succeed, they feel pride in their accomplishments. However, when they do not succeed, they control their dissatisfaction, anger, and frustration so that it does not overcome them. Instead, they use these experiences to motivate them and to continue to learn so that they can be successful in the future.

For example, female soccer players were assessed, and the research found that they had high levels of striving for perfection, hope for success, and self-serving attributions. They saw success as internal, failure as external. As a result, they had a winning mentality.[55]

## Perfectionism

Most companies who win the Malcolm Baldrige National Quality Award are not restaurants. Yet, one winner is—Rudy's Bar-B-Q—and their motto is "The Love of Excellence." They believe that quality is everything. Whether

---

55 Joachim Stoeber and Claudia Becker, "Perfectionism, achievement motives, and attribution of success and failure in female soccer players," *International Journal of Psychology* 43, no. 6 (December 2008): 980–87.

it is in ingredients or customer service, Rudy's delights guests with a memorable dining experience because their "why" is quality. They accomplish this quality by overcommunicating, overlearning, overmeasuring, and trying to be perfect—even down to the amount of lemonade to pour into a glass so that it satisfies the customer without overflowing when a lid is put on. Other companies have now come to emulate their business practices.

Overall, perfectionism is highly correlated with the hope for success and the fear of failure. These two facets are the paradoxical nature of perfectionism. It can be helpful but also quite harmful.

Attributions of healthy pursuits of excellence are related to hope and a self-serving internal attribution of success. This positive dimension results in helpful tools like high personal standards, positive evaluations of past achievement, positive expectations regarding future achievement, and higher performance. In sports, this striving is associated with an adaptive pattern of positive self-talk that helps athletic performance.

Second, and in contrast, perfectionism can include tendencies toward overly critical evaluations of one's behavior. These negative reactions come from a fear of failure and an external attribution of success. These reactions undermine athletic performance as well as performance in the business world. This negative dimension of perfectionism can include: concern over making mistakes, doubts about actions, feelings of discrepancy between expectations and results, negative reactions to mistakes, test anxiety, fear of negative evaluation, and low self-esteem.

Overall, perfectionism can be helpful when it helps to push a person to higher levels of performance, but it is harmful when it leads them to believe they are not in control or capable of performing their best.

When assessing these two facets, it is important to understand their causes. Internal circumstances are those within the person, such as natural talent and competence. External factors are those variables in the environment, such as others' talent and abilities. When you attribute success to something that you have internally, you can have positive emotions, such as pride, drive and determination, and high self-esteem. On the flip side, when you associate internally during instances of failure, you will have negative emotions, such as shame and guilt. Whether in success or failure, it is healthy to reflect on what you attribute the outcome to.

## *A Note about Pride*

People can get into a never-ending loop of analysis paralysis as teams struggle with perfection, but leaders still want team members who deliver high-quality deliverables.

When you read about perfectionism, you may be attributing the idea of "being perfect" with an individual's pride. There are two types of pride, and on a team, one is attractive and the other is a repellent. Hubristic pride is the negative, where the team member is considered a jerk. This person has a self-centered attitude and is not cognizant about other team members' contributions. The other type of pride is authentic pride, which is admirable, because it comes after an accomplishment that someone diligently worked toward. The difference between hubristic and authentic pride is humility. On a team, you see authentic pride when a team member realizes and recognizes the other team members' support and effort that they depend on to succeed.

## Teamwork Satisfaction

When errors happen, and they always do, you have to push through them with the support of your team. An African proverb says that while an individual goes fast, a team goes far.

The USWNT was playing Germany in the 1999 World Cup when Brandi Chastain accidentally scored an "own goal" due to a miscommunication. In this instance, Brandi was not subbed out. Instead, the captain verbally encouraged her. Instead of asking, "What the heck is wrong with you?" the team's approach was, "We need you; don't worry about what just happened." With this investment in her feelings and the backing by the team captain, Brandi came back after halftime and scored a key goal to tie the game. The team went on to win the game, and afterward President Bill Clinton came to the locker room with his wife and daughter to celebrate the win with the team.

## Encourage Collaborative Teamwork

There is a positive relationship between collaborative teamwork and team satisfaction. Team satisfaction is built from a foundation where each team member believes in their team's future. This belief on the team's direction is typically influenced by the degree of positivity of team members' attitudes and the level of team collaboration.

An example of a satisfied team collaborating effectively was at President George W. Bush's White House's largest public event, the annual outdoor Easter Egg Roll. It rained. The event, which typically has over forty thousand attendees, was almost cancelled. At eight thirty a.m., First Lady Laura Bush, who hosted the event, asked for it to be moved inside. In thirty minutes, her team and a host of other federal agencies who were involved had to collaborate quickly and effectively to transition the event indoors. The visitor's office, Office of the First Lady, press team, National Park Services, Office of Public Liaison, Office of Political Affairs, congressional staffers, Military Aid Office, and others worked innately together to honor every one of the forty thousand ticket holders, starting at nine a.m. The successful collaboration of each one of these teams to respond to that day's inclement weather led to an exhilarating feeling of team satisfaction. They did not disappoint thousands attending, who participated in egg roll racing with laughter. At the end of the day, one of the team members responded with her overwhelming feeling, saying, "We pulled this off together!"

## Manage Team Perceptions

Team expectations strongly influence a person's perceptions of team performance. Aligned team members' values and goals generate higher commitment to performance. Giving work a defined purpose impacts performance and team morale. Team members are enthusiastic, optimistic, and confident. Winning creates team satisfaction in sports, and revenue does the same in business. When team performance negatively impacts revenue, this indicates team performance declining, and team satisfaction subsequently falls, too. Team members know they will have to work hard to seek excellence and will have to decide whether the juice is worth the squeeze.

## Encourage Good Team Chemistry

Team chemistry relates to higher levels of teamwork satisfaction, which creates an environment where team members look forward to working together, as it is an opportunity to socialize. These healthy dynamics at work also lead to employees spending time together outside of work. When there is good chemistry, team members understand and appreciate that working efficiently together toward a joint deliverable is better and more fun than what they could have generated alone. They are recognized not only for individual contribution to the team but also for the overall team's goal accomplishments.

# Resilience

Soccer is a mental game. Coach Tony DiCicco knew this and brought in Dr. Colleen Hacker, a mental skills coach, to work with the USWNT to add another element to their preparation. She helped them gain a competitive edge, that of resilience. Having never worked with a peak performance coach before, Kristine was initially skeptical. To her credit, Dr. Hacker did not push the team into following her advice. Instead, she told them what she was offering and asked them to try it. She was there to help Kristine and her teammates set goals, manage stress, build concentration and focus, and control distractions.

Today, Kristine now counts "Hack" as one of the greatest people she knows. In 1996 before the Olympics, Dr. Hacker provided players a tape of music to listen to, which included phrases that captured each player's key goals. Kristine chose three phrases that she wanted to focus on during the game: "give me the ball," "run," and "get to the end line." By listening to these words with music before the game, she was feeling what she wanted to focus on. This visualization exercise raised each player's confidence when she stepped on the field for the Olympics. This visualization reminded her of her strengths and reinforced what was positive.

Dr. Hacker also helped the team develop their mental game in other ways. After one practice, she told them the story of the "blue car and the red car." To win a race between a blue car and red car, the blue car team had to give extra effort in every single element—driver fitness, crew pit stop efficiency, design team aerodynamics, and more—because the smallest bit of not being prepared meant the red car would win. After her talk, she gave each member on the team a blue car toy. This talk was beneficial for the team's mental approach, and Kristine still has the blue car toy in her house to remind her that even the smallest things matter!

Another tool that Dr. Hacker gave the USWNT that helped them increase their satisfaction was to teach them a simple phrase: "Leave it in the parking lot." When someone said this, it meant that the team would circle back to this thought/discussion later. This phrase enabled them to put larger, non-pressing issues aside and focus on what was critical at that moment. For peak performance, a player has to be capable of refocusing throughout the game, regardless of what just happened. You do not want to let one error beat you twice. "Park it" meant "forget the past; focus on what we need to accomplish now." It can also remind teams to not worry about the future and instead be present in the moment. Through creative solutions, Dr. Hacker built a trusting relationship with the players and developed their resilience, which nurtured team cohesion.

## Keep Your Eye on the Ball

In the business world, you must also be resilient. The economy, your company, and your career may sometimes feel like a roller coaster. You must be willing to learn, unlearn, and relearn. By keeping your eye on the ball and focusing your attention on the task at hand, you'll be able to make your comeback. It is a mental game just like any sport.

As a team member, you need to diagnose the root of your mistake and quickly address it so that you can bounce back for your team. Whenever you see a team member showing resilience, it increases the morale of the entire team. The team provides a community around you to share with and get you through the tough times. Be intentional amid the chaos.

## Uncomfortable Learning

Learning can be uncomfortable. For many, work is not conducive for making mistakes, so people avoid taking risks. A leader can create a trusting and supportive environment so individuals can feel comfortable enough to say, "I don't know," understanding that their teammates will be respectful. This type of team will always try and contribute to the well-being of the team. They have a safety net where attempts are celebrated and the amount of resilience is minimal since the fall is not far.

In order for a powerhouse to succeed with this winning mentality strategy, you will need to seek excellence, invest in teamwork satisfaction, and be resilient. In the interview that follows, you will learn more how Dr. Colleen Hacker assists her teams.

# 1:1 with Dr. Colleen Hacker

Dr. Hacker is a mental skills coach who worked with the USWNT from 1995–2007 under three different coaches. She also served on the coaching staff for the US Women's Hockey team, as well as coached individuals in the National Football League (NFL), the National Women's Soccer League (NWSL), Professional Golfers' Association (PGA), and Major League Baseball (MLB).

## How did Kristine help the USWNT have a high standard of excellence?

Kristine's impact as a person and as an elite athlete is broad and deep. There are many people who wore the national team jersey, yet her character and work ethic are unparalleled. She set the standard high for others to follow. Whether it was skill execution, hearing a coaching comment and translating it to the field, or her tireless work rate, her integrity and high standards showed in a thousand ways. Her consistent preparation before matches was painstaking in its commitment to detail and consistency, no matter the opponent or match. She went over in her mind what she needed to do, and it prepared her for excellence. For Kristine, this was an active and intentional process.

Excellence doesn't just happen on the field; it is preceded by what happens in the locker room, in the weight room, in fitness, and in mental preparation. If you want elite results, you train to make a difference when a difference is required. The margin of victory is small, and you need a player like Kristine who is a difference maker. At the end of the game, when everyone else has lead in their legs, she was flying down the left flank and delivering the perfect ball into the box so that someone could finish it and score! She trained to be her best when her best was needed.

For an international match in Portland, Oregon, her sponsor manufactured a pair of one-of-a-kind gold shoes for her 200th cap. Very few players in history ever achieve a two-hundred-cap career, let alone receive the honor of custom-made gold shoes. Fans of the game understood soccer history and the unique place that Kristine held. Her legacy was large, and her teammates, who knew her best of all, were filled with respect and appreciation for her and what she accomplished, and they actually carried her off the field. I don't honestly recall another player to ever receive that honor!

For many professional athletes, there is a significant disconnect between what the world "thinks" of them and who they really are. I work with and know many elite performers in a wide range of achievement domains, and I often joke that I liked them better before I actually met them! Not Kristine. She loved what she did and was out there to do her job to the highest standards each and every day. She was the consummate teammate and was as consistent on the field as she was off the field. Kristine treated others (teammates, fans, opponents) and the game with the utmost respect. Everyone admired her.

## What is an example of teamwork satisfaction?

At the 1999 World Cup, when Kristine was exhausted and the team was exhausted from playing a full ninety minutes and two overtimes against China, she had the poise, discipline, skill, and maturity to do her job at one of *the* most critical moments of the entire game. Her job was to protect the post on the corner kick late in that match. It was her mental toughness under unspeakable pressure that allowed her to do her job when the demand for excellence was most critical. In my mind, there is not a US World Cup victory and no penalty kicks after overtime without Lil's header on the post during that corner kick. In fact, at the first team meeting in 2000 after the World Cup, I brought Kristine to the front of the room, along with the two captains. I handed the leaders a measuring tape and asked them to measure Kristine's forehead. It is 4.5 inches, if you were wondering. The 1999 World Cup, played on a field 120 yards long and 80 yards wide, was won by 4.5 inches . . . the width of Kristine's forehead! That is a small margin of victory indeed. I then told the team to pay attention to what leads to victory . . . attention to detail and doing your job 100 percent of the time.

## Why is resilience important?

While a psychologist is clinical in focus and works with issues like depression, a mental performance coach works with individuals to produce a peak performance by focusing on psychological skills like imagery, concentration control, confidence, and handling pressure, to name a few. Like all athletes and teams, the US National Team highlights training the four pillars, including:

- **Technical:** passing, shooting, heading, etc.

- **Tactical:** offensive and defensive strategies

- **Physiological:** strength training, aerobic and anaerobic conditioning, sleep, nutrition, and recovery

- **Psychological:** mindfulness, pregame preparation, handling errors, mental toughness, activation control, self-talk, confidence, etc.

All Olympic athletes have strong technical, tactical, and physiological games. What sets the elite players apart is the psychological—their mental preparedness. After a stinging loss, for example, a team realizes they are good enough physically but not quite getting it done in competition and when it counts the most. Rather than a Pollyanna approach of "hugs and kisses," this is fertile ground to realize that, if you "keep doing what you have been doing, you will keep getting what you have been getting." There is a Zen proverb that says, "I have nothing to give you, if your cup is full. Only when you empty your cup can something new be provided." A team has to want to learn and grow in order to develop and improve. It has to seek answers. It has to desire to grow and change.

Kristine would be the first to say that she was part of a group of champions. She didn't do it alone. In fact, a commitment to excellence was *the* prevailing ethos on the national team. In fact, I shared with the team two mantras that captured that confidence, preparation, and commitment to the highest standards. One was, "This is the team. Now is the time." And the other was, "What we need, we have." Both were meant to remind the players that no one in the world had trained harder or was more prepared, talented, and resilient than they were. They expected to succeed and they did consistently, winning or at least finishing in the top three of every world event in the era in which Kristine played.

## *Tactics for Your Team*

A powerhouse needs to seize a winning mentality by seeking excellence, investing in teamwork satisfaction, and being resilient. It is important to seek excellence so your team has a winning attitude and a high bar for quality standards. You should also invest in teamwork satisfaction, because when you do this, team performance improves. Finally, you want to be resilient so you can bounce back after any setbacks.

> How can you cultivate a winning mentality on your own team? How will you:
>
> **1.** Give the extra effort needed for success?
>
> **2.** Believe your team's impact is effective?
>
> **3.** Persevere when the going gets tough?

"There is always time for a high five and a laugh. Playing with some of the best in the world like Abby Wambach, you show your support in so many ways," Kristine said. This game was in Faro, Portugal, on March 15, 2006. (Credit: Brad Smith/isiphotos.com)

# Doing What Is Right

*"Ethics goes into the development of every single team,
as it is about trying to create the ethos for what
your company is about and what its intention is."*

—Abby Wambach

The thirteenth winning tactic for building a powerhouse is to do what is right. Teams make continuous decisions that impact their team as well as those around them. On many of these decisions, the wider path is easier to take, yet the narrow path is where few choose to go because it is harder. Make the decision to do the right thing.

Before Kristine got pregnant with her first child, she had played in 85 percent of the USWNT games. During her career of twenty-three years, she did not receive compensation for several of those years, only receiving a modest per diem of $10 a day when they were together as a team. It wasn't until 1995 that the team finally realized they had the right to be paid. This is when the players began fighting for what was right. As the years went on, these players, who were now world champions and Olympic gold medalists, were appreciative of the financial increase, even if the amount was minimal compared to other professional athletes. Still, each time they negotiated and proved their worth, they stood up for what was right—right for them and right for future generations.

The US victory at the Women's World Cup in 1999 set an attendance record for women's sporting events. *Sports Illustrated* wrote, "With an estimated 40 million US viewers, the Cup final was the most watched soccer match in the history of network television, and the turnout of 90,185 at the Rose Bowl was the largest ever to watch a women's sporting event." These feelings were supported by the FIFA organization, who said the championship match was the most watched soccer match in American history. As a result of the women's team's success, soccer emerged as the most visible women's team sport in North America. The players became household names and made guest appearances on ABC's *Good Morning America*, NBC's *Today,* and the *Late Show with David Letterman.*[56]

Despite all of these appearances and their widespread popularity, the women are still fighting for fair pay. Fast forward to the 2015 World Cup when twenty-five million viewers tuned in to see the US beat Japan 5–2, their third World Cup Championship. Comparing that to the year before at the 2014 World Cup, "The men's bonus for being named to the final 23-player World Cup roster was $55,000 each; the women earned $15,000 each."[57]

## Why Doing What Is Right Is Important

Today, Kristine wants and expects that her two daughters, Sidney and Jordan, will be paid fairly regardless of their career choice. Whether they are professional soccer players or firefighters or business executives, she wants them to be paid equally.

It may not be popular, supported, or easy, yet team members want to be on diverse, ethical teams that overcome adversity.

## Overcoming Adversity

The Olympic games provide unparalleled opportunities for athletes to gain international visibility. This worldwide exposure can lead to corporate sponsorships and endorsements for individual Olympians, which is a necessity for many

---

56  Nancy E. Spencer, Lisa R. McClung, "Women and Sport in the 1990s: Reflections on 'Embracing Stars, Ignoring Players,'" *Journal of Sport Management* 15, no. 4 (October 2001): 318–349, https://journals.humankinetics.com/doi/abs/10.1123/jsm.15.4.318.

57  Evan Davis, "Women Earn the Glory While Men Earn the Money in U.S. Soccer," FiveThirtyEight.com, March 31, 2016, https://fivethirtyeight.com/features/women-earn-the-glory-while-men-earn-the-money-in-u-s-soccer/.

athletes' survival. Women's participation at the Olympics continues to increase as a percent of the competitors, and the 1996 games were no exception. In fact, the 1996 games in Atlanta, Georgia, were the first time in the history of the games that women could participate in the sport of soccer, a privilege these women prepared for each and every day.

Yet, the USWNT risked their Olympic dreams by standing up for what was right. They saw inequity in contracts. Nine of what the *Los Angeles Times* called the "most prestigious" team members, including Kristine, refused to go into training camp before the 1996 Olympics over a contract dispute. This was taking a stand for what they believed in, as well as establishing better conditions for future generations of players. Thus, after finding common ground on their contract, they overcame this adversity, which helped cement this team together for victory on the field and off of it.

Can you imagine when your team decides to jeopardize your lifelong dream of being in the Olympics in order to do what is right for future generations of women playing sports after you? It took team resolve to make the decision to risk a dream for societal good, and this extremely tight dedication to the team's purpose carried over to the field when they played the games. Despite all of this adversity, Kristine and her teammates were able to take home the first ever women's soccer gold medal. They won that gold medal because a group of women stood up for what is right, and they were also talented, dedicated, hardworking, and had a love for the game and each other.

Fighting for women's participation has finally paid off. According to the Olympics official website: "The number of women athletes at the Olympic Games is approaching 50 percent. Since 2012, women have participated in every Olympic sport at the Games. All new sports to be included in the Games must contain women's events."

## Minimize Adversity

In the business world, similar to Kristine's team at the 1996 Olympics, the environment is continuously changing and things can get tough. These complicated challenges and demands can sink a team. When a team encounters setback after setback, they could quickly spiral downward. Instead, a team must come together to face a common enemy instead of turning on each other internally.

When an interviewer asked a well-respected professor who the best teacher he ever had was, his answer was "failure." Although failure can be a difficult teacher, the team has to take responsibility so they can learn and grow from the situation. It is not a blame game. Minimizing adversity is a matter of taking responsibility by those who have the strength to be accountable. Healthy organizations analyze the experience and outcome of their teams, understanding what they could have done better to prevent the adversity or mitigate the impact of the issue so they can be better prepared moving forward.

## Jump Back In

With a continuous improvement mindset, your team performance will be on a never-ending ascension. Teams know they have executive support to overcome adversity when leadership believes the team can overcome any roadblock, be adaptable to changes, and perform to achieve their team goals. There is no self-pity. Instead, the team can be flexible and adaptable to the new context that their leadership suggests. After all, the team needs to "jump back in" to be ready to perform. When a team does overcome adversity, it increases their bond. After working through the adversity, leaders re-communicate their purpose, their goals, and the overall team direction to keep the team's eye on the ball by reminding team members of their goals and objectives.

## Diversity

So even after three World Cup championships, the pay between men and women soccer players was still significantly different. Not only does this impact morale during their playing days, but later, at the end of their career when the players would look at the years they spent on a professional team, a stark reality would emerge—male professional athletes are financially set for life if they have been conservative with their expenditures because they are adequately paid for their work. Female professional athletes, who have systematically been undervalued, have no such resources. They often have to find a new source of income.

Soccer is the only professional sport where male and female athletes have the same employer, the United States Soccer Federation (USSF). Because they have the same employer, when we talk about equal remuneration between men and women, the Equal Pay Act is uniquely relevant when examining soccer in the US. For an equal pay complaint, there must be examples of equal work.[58]

The USWNT historically played more games, won twice as many games, and has recently brought in more revenue. The amount of money the USWNT earns for winning a World Cup is a fraction of what the winning country's men's team earns. In addition, men play for both club and country, where the club pays most of their lucrative salary.[59] The women's professional league is in the early stages of growing the game with modest salaries. The USWNT players achieved in spite of the adversity they had to overcome. Yet, their platform today is advocating for "doing what is right" in compensating for future generations of players. While their successes on the field have been significant, they are striving for something greater—societal change for equality.

## Equal

Soccer is not the only business that struggles with implementing equal pay for all of its employees. Although numbers show that the incoming workforce is about half women, the numbers start decreasing from there. Women receive less coaching, take longer to get promoted, and have lower salaries. This is highlighted when you look at the number of female managers, the number of female CEOs, and even the number of females on corporate boards.

Even if there is still a long way to go toward equality between genders in the workforce, this battle for equality should not end until all citizens are compensated fairly. Wage equality is not vague. It is a measurable and attainable goal.

Many employees do not know if their company has wage equality because salaries are kept private, and employees are told that sharing their salary is grounds for termination.

However, there is a historical pattern of paying women less than men. For many companies, this is not acknowledged until a lawsuit requires a statistical model review of their salaries per position level. Through this discovery,

---

58  Garris, Morgan, Wilkes, "Soccernomics: Salaries for World Cup Soccer Athletes," *International Journal of the Academic Business World* (2017).

59  Garris, Morgan, Wilkes, "Soccernomics: Salaries for World Cup Soccer Athletes," *International Journal of the Academic Business World* (2017).

women are reimbursed for years of not being paid what they should have been making. Before a lawsuit, companies should address diversity and pay equality during talent acquisition. By implementing policies for prospect diversity slates and hiring goals, a company can funnel equality into their workforce. After that, it is a question of retention and promotion.

This structure mitigates the faster promotions, increased coaching, and higher salaries that happen if left unchecked. Finally, companies need to prioritize diversity at the top—the C-Suite and board membership. If no leader at the top advocates for whom they are representing, then that means there is also no leader to be a role model for others in the organization.

## Diverse Opportunities

Kristine was born the year before the United States passed Title IX of the Education Amendments Act of 1972. This federal law states that "no person in the United States shall, on the basis of sex, be excluded from participation in, be denied the benefits of, or be subjected to discrimination under any education program or activity receiving Federal financial assistance." This groundbreaking legislation opened up high school, university, and all sorts of intercollegiate programs to women. The number of female players increased from hundreds of thousands to millions.

Title IX eventually helped many professional women's leagues emerge, including soccer, basketball, ice hockey, softball, volleyball, baseball, and football. The popularity and need for these programs dispels the notion that women's place in sports is "in the stands, not on the court." Coach Tony DiCicco summed up this idea when he said, "Society often positions women to just fit in. We coach them, however, to stand out, to make a difference, and for women that can be an incredibly empowering experience."[60] DiCicco believed in using his privilege as a white male sports professional to help lead the efforts of gender equality by encouraging his soccer players to use their sport as a platform to promote their cause.

While Title IX has helped women, the concept of diversity extends beyond gender: it includes racial minorities, individuals with disabilities, and others. We advocate for all "diversity," just like policies besides Title IX have done.

---

60    Tony DiCicco, Colleen Hacker, *Catch Them Being Good* (New York: Penguin Books, 2002).

## Encourage Diversity

Your business can find great value in having a diverse team. Just as a sports team would fail if everyone on it excelled at only a single skill, so would your organization have gaps and weaknesses. From a diversity perspective, doing what is right means removing challenges that may come from gender, ethnicity, or any other division where people have been treated unequally.

Diversity can be visible differences in age, gender, and/or race, but it can also mean providing opportunities for those with different knowledge, skills, and abilities developed from different work experiences and personality traits. When a team has varied perspectives, the door opens to new ideas and learning. The team can then be more creative and innovative in its solutions, achieving optimum results with better decisions. Diversity also helps prevent group think. Diverse teams may contribute to higher group performance than those composed of similar members.

It's not enough just to provide opportunities for observable different characteristics such as gender, age, or ethnicity; we encourage companies to keep supporting these valuable members of their team throughout their careers. A diverse workforce will help your team succeed!

## A Note on Centered-Set Thinking

It may seem like introducing diversity to your teams may make them more difficult to manage effectively. However, because your teams will have a common goal, they likely will have other common values that allow them to identify with each other.

We spoke with a pastor of a multidenominational church that has many backgrounds and faiths present during worship service about how he manages the diverse viewpoints. For the church to be successful, how do seemingly different people find common ground? He said, "We focus on being 'centered set' instead of 'bounded set' to incorporate many faith backgrounds."

*continued*

The pastor was referring to a theory originally proposed over twenty-five years ago by Paul Hiebert. Essentially, a "bounded set" group uses borders, fences, and walls to determine if a person is "in" or "outside of" the community. If you are "in," then there are requirements made on you. Basically, it is a perspective that focuses on what divides people rather than what unites them.

The opposing perspective is what defines a "centered-set" group—or team. This perspective determines "what unites us," a core value that binds all together. Everyone is part of this team, even if some are closer to the center than others. There are no walls, and no one is excluded.

Centered-set thinking helps teams with diverse membership thrive. They work better together based on the common ground between each member. It is a shared mindset, a common identity.

A centered-set leader tightens down on the center—what binds the team together—and enables the individual to be strong with who they are as a person. The individual is set free to use their skillset and capability as a resource for the team to be successful. Each individual, regardless of their differences, strives to be the best they can be for the team.

## The Importance of Ethics

A study of Belgium soccer players assessed their coaches being effective in counteracting unethical behavior, as they are responsible for creating a safe sports environment to affect the players' moral behavior. The coach works the closest with the team, having the most time and influence over a player. The leader models behavior to influence subordinates, who observe and imitate. The soccer players received ethical guidance from their coaches, and learned from them what is expected, rewarded, and punished. Thus, coaches should train players on soccer tactics while also being conscious of their impact on ethical choices.[61]

---

61  Bram Constandt, Els De Waegeneer, and Annick Willem, "Coach Ethical Leadership in Soccer Clubs: An Analysis of Its Influence on Ethical Behavior," *Journal of Sport Management* 32, no. 3 (May 2018): 185–98.

## Ethical Leadership

Companies who are unethical can be found all over the news: Enron's massive accounting fraud, Bernard Madoff's Ponzi scheme, Lehman Brothers' bankruptcy, and Volvo's emission scandal each made headlines over the past couple decades. Each of these companies suffered from failed business leadership that engaged in unethical behavior. Even worse, they often created workplace culture conditions that required employees to act unethically in order to succeed.

A business team member needs an ethical conscience, and a team leader needs to influence others to do what is right and to act with moral standards. A leader should model what is right for their employees and consider fairness, transparency, and honesty in their interactions with team members. Despite the pressure to put profit ahead of people, an ethical leader should try to ensure that all assignments are mutually beneficial between the employee and the company, and fairly compensated.

## Ethical Behavior

An employee needs tools to check their behavior against what is right. On a team, members look to others and the leader for what to do, indicating loyalty or gratitude. On a larger level, your business's culture is shaped by this perception of what ethically correct behavior is, as well as how issues should be handled. As a leader you can help your team develop an internal ethical framework so that they can judge a situation and then choose how to act.

One business uses a framework called the "3M Rule." In their culture, the 3 Ms stand for Mother, Mentor, or Media. Team members are instructed to ask themselves, "Would you do what you are doing if your mother, your mentor, or the media were watching?" If they determine that whatever they are deciding to do would not be appropriate in front of the 3Ms, then the team member should reconsider why they are doing that activity at all.

You can transform the world by creating an ethical culture in your organization. No one graduates from college thinking they will take a job and make an unethical decision, yet that commonly happens. First, strive for moral consistency across all areas of your life to set the right/wrong example for everyone you encounter. Second, protect your personal honor, as socially acceptable behavior misconduct is unfortunately rampant in today's business. Finally, your moral compass will tell you when you need to stand up to social injustice.[62]

## The USWNT Is an Ethical Example

The US Women's National Soccer team has always been involved in fighting for what they believe in. The USWNT has fought for their rights, for women's rights, and for the rights of future generations. As a team, they are playing and fighting for societal change and justice.

These larger efforts were first recognized when *Sports Illustrated* awarded the team the 1999 Sportsperson of the Year after they won the World Cup against China. This annual honor chooses an athlete or team "whose performance that year most embodies the spirit of sportsmanship and achievement." The US Women's National Team joins the 1980 US Olympic Hockey Team as the only teams so honored in the forty-six-year history of the award. Not only did *Sports Illustrated* capture the 1999 World Cup Champions but they also made a special cover featuring the World Cup Champions of 2015.

Boston Consulting Group agrees, saying that the team is "notable not just for its victories. The players redefined the role of women in sports, fighting for gender equality, equal pay, and the reputation of women's soccer."

In order for a powerhouse to do what is right, you will need a leader like Abby Wambach. She is famous for how she overcame adversity, what she is doing now to seek diversity, and why being ethical is so critical for sports and other organizations going forward.

## 1:1 with Abby Wambach

Abby Wambach won the US Soccer Athlete of the Year award six times while she played on the USWNT from 2003 to 2015. She scored the most goals (184) and was the 2011 Associated Press Athlete of the Year, and the 2012 FIFA World Player of the Year.

---

62  Lawrence Kohlberg, Stages of Moral Development (1971), https://www. psychologynoteshq.com/kohlbergstheory/.

## What is the best advice you have for overcoming adversity?

When I was on the Youth National Team, I had the opportunity to visit the USWNT's locker room while they were preparing for the 1996 Olympics. I was surprised to see a picture taped next to the exit door. It was the Norwegian national team, celebrating after having just beaten the USA in the 1995 World Cup. Having this visible in their space showed me that the USWNT confronted their failure and then used that failure as fuel to prepare and win the 1996 Olympic gold! It is a mindset shift that taught me to use failure to grow.

As a young player, I also learned from the veteran players' experience and wisdom. I learned a relentless pursuit of excellence. This was our defining pillar for what makes a team successful and how it can overcome adversity. This culture has been passed down from team to team and is the central theme that runs through every USWNT player. We don't want to just be a team; we want to win. That is a full tenet of who we are. Full stop. Winning is about many things, not just scoring more goals than the other team. It is also about representing the country, and it is how well we play.

A successful team constantly challenges you to be better. Our drive meant that we would argue and get pissed off at each other, but at the end of the day, we still had to meet the goals set by our leadership to realize our dream of attaining a championship.

## How can an organization effectively seek diversity?

There are benefits for any organization to have diversity and inclusion. Even if women are getting entry-level positions, there are very few women around the C-Suite table making decisions. If your consumer base is the world, your leadership base needs to reflect that. What do you want your company to be in the future? Figure out who you are with a mission statement as a company. The next generation wants to be a part of a company that has a cause, not just capital gains.

To get to a solution, you need multiple perspectives. No one else has lived your specific life, and it gives you a different perspective than everyone else. When you walk onto a team, there are invisible team norms. These are certain expectations and requirements that you need to bring to the table every time. So many times people can't get beyond themselves, because they can't work with someone with different political views or who isn't similar to them. No matter how different you are from your team members, you have to find a way to respect your team members around you, because they showed up.

The true test of a leader is inspiring the next generation of leaders, and that is when you truly step into your leadership role. It is an honor. I wrote *Wolfpack* and founded Wolfpack Endeavor to teach the elite champion mindset for high-potential women in the corporate world and beyond.

## How does a company act ethically?

As the saying goes, "One bad apple spoils the whole bunch." Ethics goes into the development of every single team, as it is about trying to create the ethos for what your company is about and what its intention is. It is a leader who acts democratically, with whom they are serving and employing. Maturity and wisdom build a strong foundation of who you are as a company.

When I think about the USWNT, I think our ethics were shaped by all the non-negotiables, or what we wouldn't do, because we were representing an entire country. Some coaches create this foundation of team, culture, excellence, and ethics. Other coaches can't deploy this. The team must then hold true to their values, which starts with the respect and trust that built the team. You never sway away from them, nor do you ever sweep them under the rug. The integrity must last. A team must create these non-negotiables, and it has to be talked about by the team leadership from the top down. Then, it has to be accepted by the team from the bottom up so that it is embodied by every single person.

## *Tactics for Your Team*

When doing the right thing, powerhouses overcome adversity by confronting their failures. These teams should seek diversity for the positive business impact by finding their centered set. A powerhouse is ethical, clearly knowing right from wrong and working to transform its culture so that it can effect societal change.

Consider applying these three principles to your own organization. How will you:

**1.** Learn from obstacles and failure?

**2.** Assemble diverse teams with centered common ground?

**3.** Act with integrity?

*Alex Morgan and Megan Rapinoe celebrate their gold medals from the 2012
Olympics. "I love this photo," Kristine said. "When you win and are
Olympic gold medalists, it is hard to hide the happiness." (Credit: John Todd/
isiphotos.com)*

# Afterword

Our intent writing *Powerhouse* was twofold: we wanted to share Kristine's journey with the USWNT, and we wanted to share high-performance teamwork tactics that you could apply to help develop your organization. Within the key areas of **T**ransform, **E**mpower, **A**chieve, and **M**otivate, reflect on the thirteen tactics for your team, and prioritize the top two that your team can work on immediately.

Every team has opportunities to build a powerhouse. Now that you have prepared, it is time to practice and perform. Once you implement these strategies, your teamwork will have a powerful impact on your organization's results. Remember, always believe.

To further develop your organization's teamwork, please contact:

- Kristine's Speaking: kristinelilly13.com
- Lynette and John's Speaking: JohnGillisJr.com
- "How to Build a Powerhouse" workshop: LeadershipX.com
- TeamFirst Soccer Clinic: TeamFirstSoccerAcademy.com

Since Kristine's retirement, the USWNT continues to win. By establishing these thirteen tactics, the team remains successful even when the roster continuously changes. To wrap up this book, we asked the USWNT co-captains who represent the next generation to reflect on these thirteen powerhouse tactics. Megan Rapinoe and Alex Morgan joined the team "green" when Kristine was "gray."

# 1:1 with Alex Morgan and Megan Rapinoe

Alex Morgan and Megan Rapinoe, USWNT co-captains, together won the 2012 Olympic gold in London and the 2015 World Cup Championship in Canada. Alex is a two-time US Soccer Athlete of the Year, and wrote *The Kicks* children's book series. In addition, she is a Global Athlete Ambassador for UNICEF. Megan won the 2011 ESPY Award for "Best Play of the Year" for her assist to Abby Wambach in the World Cup that year. Her company, Rapinoe SC, has a mission to "inspire and celebrate the physical and emotional exploration of what it means to Be Your Best You."

## Can you speak to the importance of selecting the right team members?

**Megan Rapinoe (MR):** Trying out for the USWNT is an intense environment. Not only are you fighting for your position on the team to do what you love to do, you are also fighting for your livelihood, as there is not much money for a soccer player to make if they aren't on the USWNT. However, once the team is created, everyone has a common bond of going through try-outs so there's a feeling of teamwork. You know that each player next to you made it for a reason and they are highly qualified. This is a core strength of the team from the very beginning.

As you transition from being a young player to a veteran, you have the capacity to do more for the team. If you have staying power and have been on the team for a while, then you are doing something right, as it takes grit and self-confidence to remain on the team. You have to perform at the expected high level. It is a balance to lead, as you also need to stay on the top of your game as well to fight for your roster spot. Still, veteran players often become leaders, and take on the responsibility of putting the new team members under their wings. These new players see how veterans operate, how they approach the game day-to-day, how to grind through a bad game, and how they demonstrate a certain level of professionalism.

## How do you and your teammates align with your team's overall team direction?

**Alex Morgan (AM):** While the USWNT is at the top of the rankings, we are not dominating other teams like we used to. The top ten teams are much closer in talent now. This requires a lot of strategy and tactical preparation on our part.

Team sports build character, develop personality, and teach time management. You have to get to know your team members' strengths and weaknesses and fill the role that your team needs from you. You have to trust that they will pick you up when you fall. When you get to the highest stage, you must put your own selfish needs aside. I thrive in a team environment because I love to celebrate with my teammates when we win.

## Can you share what you do to challenge yourself, so you can keep scoring goals?

**AM:** Before there was even a women's professional league, I wrote a note to my mom when I was seven years old, "When I grow up, I want to be a professional soccer player. Love, Ali Cat." Since then, I have developed and improved—I still have yet to reach my full potential. Outside of our team training, I work on what I need to help set me up to accomplish my personal goals. I am specific with what I want to work on each and every month.

When your personal goal and the team goal are aligned, they maximize each other. When I step on the field, I have a goal set in my mind, whether that is scoring a goal or maintaining possession of the ball. This depends on what the team needs, and what my role is.

## How does a coach set the foundation and expectation for the rest of the team?

**AM:** Leading the team goes beyond selecting the best players; it is about managing the players' egos and personalities. There cannot be negative energy within the group, as you spend a lot of time with these people. Then, a leader has to tactically prepare for each game. Every person has to be on the same page. While each team has a certain style, you have to be willing to adjust as necessary. The leader has a large role in the team's success.

The leader has to be very clear with players about their individual roles in order for the team to mesh well. A mental skills coach helps us bridge the gaps, to help the team understand that each of us comes from a different upbringing, a different part of the country, and a different skillset to bring to the team. We are playing at a different level, and everyone wants to be on the starting line. Regardless if you are a starter or reserve, there is a feeling on the team that everyone supports one another. We consider each other sisters, yet we do not have to be best friends. We have a common goal that we are working toward. This is an incredible feeling, one that you can't teach or prepare for. This understanding of what being on the USWNT means that it has been passed down from when Lil was on the team. It is just the way it is, an awesome mentality, a way of being.

## Can you talk a little about what it is like for you to lead your team and how that has affected you as a person?

**AM:** I have not changed who I am since I became one of the USWNT co-captains. I am supposed to be the voice of the team, and to do that effectively I need to know the pulse of the team. My job is to check with each player and make sure that their voice is being heard, regardless if they are vocal are not. I want younger team members to know that I am approachable, instead of them feeling like I am intimidating. I am not afraid to speak up, as I encourage players before the game, yet I don't want to talk just to talk. There has to be meaning and purpose behind what I say.

## Can you share what it was like playing on an international team?

**MR:** I played one year in Lyon, France. It was a different team environment, where we would practice and then go home. Their culture is more insular and reserved. I was used to off-the-field camaraderie and having fun, which contributes to on-the-field success. Now, with so many foreign players playing professional soccer in the US for NWSL, we try to include them in the social mix with off-the-field activities.

## Did your overall sense of teamwork and desire to succeed have an impact on how you prepped for each game?

**MR:** To prepare for the games, you have to be fit. Fitness is hard for everyone, but you have to just quit complaining and do it. I was lucky as a younger player to learn from Lil. She was a professional, yet had a positive attitude and a fun approach. As you become a veteran player, you have a responsibility to mentor the younger players. If they have a bad game or a tough meeting with the coach, you are there to let them know it is going to be OK. Other times, you let them figure it out by grinding through it. It is a balance.

## What steps do you and others on the team take to improve communications?

**AM:** Players find their role and voice on the team. You never want too many people speaking up at once, as there needs to be a balance. We had a great vocal leader in Abby Wambach, yet there was a void in that role when she left. Our team lifted up another player to be that vocal presence that our team needed.

## How do you handle conflict on the team?

**AM:** Our team definitely has conflict, but some ways are better at addressing it than others. The best way to handle conflict is to address it player to player. When you involve too many other players, the conflict becomes a dark hole. It becomes much larger than necessary. Everyone doesn't need to get along at all times, but the team needs a common understanding. This is the base for working things out.

## Your team has a really great chemistry. Can you speak to that and how it affects your game?

**MR:** The team knows collectively what they are trying to do. Because there are clearly defined roles, each player is setting up other players so that the team can succeed. There are so many variables in a game, and each player has to make a choice with the ball. The team is like one brain, and each team member is an extension. When you look back, you can see how the team grew and how it made it through a struggle. Then when you win, it is the greatest feeling—and you get to share it with your teammates!

## How do you balance your unique talent with your teammates?

**MR:** My life motto is: "Be something special that no one else can be, and do that to the best of your ability. No one can be you."

You have to bring your special thing—your unique thing—to the team. Keep your individual freedom, personality, and express yourself. You can't compare yourself to anyone else, as they are better at another aspect of the game. You need to be something that no one else can be. Realize that no one can do what you can do, and you can't do what they do. Resist the temptation of trying to be someone else, and realize that you are unique.

Still, there needs to be a balance of plugging in what you bring to the game and meshing it with what is best for the team. Everyone is finding their own individual creativity in the greater whole. Use your skills and capabilities to help and serve the team. You give up a little bit of the individual to gain more as a team. This is so much greater than what you could do on your own.

## How does your team cultivate a winning mindset?

**MR:** Our team has always had faith. Even when we were losing with just two minutes left in the game, we had confidence that our team would pull it out. This winning mentality came from the collective experience of the team, who had won multiple championships. During tough times, team members supported each other. Our team had a grit and determination, as we had been there before and knew we could get through it.

## Any final advice for the reader on how to be a good teammate and how to navigate those challenging situations?

**MR:** When you have a strong conviction about things, you stand up for what you think is right. Having hard conversations is not really a problem for me, even though the other position is in a position of power that goes against you. You have to be open to having conversations and hearing other points of view, as I know that others are not going to think the same thing as I do. There are negative impacts, yet I know it was impactful to move the conversation forward. Live your life with what you think is best.

# About the Authors

**Kristine Lilly** is an expert on effective teamwork. She consults with organizations, providing lessons gleaned from her remarkable career as a professional athlete. Lilly played midfielder for the United States Women's National Soccer Team for over twenty-three years. This included five FIFA World Cups and three Olympic Games. She was inducted into the US Olympic Hall of Fame in 2012 and the US Soccer Hall of Fame in 2014. Before that, she won four national championships at The University of North Carolina.

Kristine lives outside Boston with her husband, David Heavey, a Brookline firefighter. They "team together" to raise two amazing daughters, Sidney and Jordan.

*Photo Credit: CaseyPhotography.net*

**Dr. John Gillis, Jr.** facilitates executive leadership development using a dynamic business simulation for LeadershipX. He has worked for numerous companies globally as a management consultant. He did his doctoral work at the University of Pennsylvania's Graduate School of Education and Wharton Business School. He lives in Austin, Texas, with his wife Lynette and their four children: Jack, Rylan, Caroline, and Mary Claire.

*Photo Credit: Tara Pottichen*

**Dr. Lynette Gillis** earned her PhD at the University of Texas in corporate strategy and organizational behavior, completing a dissertation on networks and teams. As a professor at Concordia University, she taught strategy, leadership, management, and ethics. She also served as dean of the College of Business. Currently, she serves as the associate provost, leading academics across diverse disciplines and colleges.

*Photo Credit: Westlake Photography*